GET BUSY LIVING

GET BUSY LIVING

A Personal Game Plan
to Unleash Your True Potential

ERIC TRAUGH

HOUNDSTOOTH
PRESS

The information in this book is not intended to be a substitute for the professional advice of physicians, psychiatrists, financial advisors, physical trainers, or dieticians. Readers should consult with their professional advisors in all matters relating to their life. In the event you choose to use any of the information in this book for yourself, you are prescribing for yourself, which is your constitutional right, but neither the author nor publisher can be held responsible for any consequences alleged to have been caused, directly or indirectly, by the information contained in this book. Don't worry, there aren't any more big words in this book.

COPYRIGHT © 2023 ERIC TRAUGH
All rights reserved.

GET BUSY LIVING
A Personal Game Plan to Unleash Your True Potential

FIRST EDITION

ISBN   978-1-5445-4334-5 *Paperback*
        978-1-5445-4335-2 *Ebook*

In memory of Darin Hanks (February 12, 1968–July 24, 2021)

Uncle Darin taught me how to fish. He made everyone laugh. A best friend who will always be remembered.

CONTENTS

OUR MISSION 11
WELCOME TO ERIC ISLAND 13
RULES FOR SUCCESS 19

PART I: QUIT BAD HABITS AND ADDICTIONS
THREE TYPES OF BAD HABITS 27
THE PROCESS OF QUITTING 31
IDENTIFY YOUR PROBLEM 33
FIND YOUR TRIGGERS 37
IDENTIFY THE EXCUSES YOU ARE MAKING 41
MAKE A PROS AND CONS LIST 47
KEEP TRACK OF YOUR FAILURES 51
LAST THOUGHTS ON QUITTING 53
FORM YOUR GAME PLAN TO QUIT 59

PART II: CREATE A QUALITY LIFESTYLE
FINANCIAL 67
PHYSICAL 73
CLEAN UP YOUR MESS! 85
YOU (OR YOUR PASSIONS) 95

PART III: GAME PLAN FOR WINNING LIFE
STEP 1: REVISIT YOUR LIST OF F. P. MESSY IDEAS................. 109
STEP 2: ASK YOURSELF QUESTIONS 111
STEP 3: SET PERIODIC GOALS 115
STEP 4: CREATE A MISSION STATEMENT AND MANTRAS....123
GBL PLAN: EXAMPLE...125

**PART IV: FINDING YOUR PASSION AND
THOUGHTS ON HAPPINESS**
FINDING YOUR PASSION..139
THOUGHTS ON HAPPINESS..149
THE END...OF THE BEGINNING 159
AN INVITATION TO THE GET BUSY LIVING CLUB!.................167
A SHORT LIST OF THANK YOUS..169
LIST OF RECOMMENDED BOOKS 173
ABOUT THE AUTHOR..179

> "*It comes down to a simple choice. Get busy living, or get busy dying.*"
>
> —ANDY (TIM ROBBINS),
> *THE SHAWSHANK REDEMPTION*

OUR MISSION

Most self-improvement books I read seem focused on the corporate world. Not everyone has a nine-to-five schedule. I wanted to create a plan anyone could use anytime, anywhere. Stay-at-home parents, nurses, doctors, pilots, janitors, law enforcement officers, or students. The list is endless, but it does not discriminate. If you have a nine-to-five job, but you feel like it takes up sixteen hours of your day—nine-to-fivers, this is for you as well.

Our mission is to form a plan you can start today, follow for the rest of your life, and maximize your potential as a human.

This is your guide to winning at life and finding *your* true happiness (not someone else's idea of happiness).

Most self-help books are the same. They repeat the same things, quote the same authors, and use the same statistics and stories. My book has no quotes, feel-good stories, or scientific explanations. There are no page-filling studies that tell you what percentage of rats who become addicted to Cheetos will also suffer from orange paws and whiskers (97.9 percent). If you are a rat who is reading this, I would love to meet you someday. However, if you are a human like I am, let's forget the statistics about how the average person or animal acts. I have never felt like a normal person. I've always felt different. If you feel this way, if nothing seems to work for you like it does for other people, if you have crazy thoughts in your head, welcome to my world.

OBJECTIVES

Part I: Quit Bad Habits and Addictions.

Part II: Create a Quality Lifestyle.

Part III: Game Plan for Winning Life.

Part IV: Finding Your Passion and Thoughts on Happiness.

WELCOME TO ERIC ISLAND

I had a great childhood growing up in Columbus, Ohio. I couldn't have asked for two better parents. I am very fortunate to have them. I was very quiet and shy, although somehow popular, I guess because I played sports. I was a pretty good kid. I was even in STAMP, Stay Tobacco-Free Athlete Mentor Program, where I would teach younger kids the negative effects of tobacco. So how the hell did I find myself, a few years later, with a beer and cigarette in my hand, wondering why my life was so messed up? Not knowing what I was going to do with my life nor having any desire to be anything at all? Later, after I became a pilot, I still wondered why my life was so different. Why couldn't I be like everyone else and want to get married, have kids, and live a normal life? Why couldn't I be a God-fearing Christian like the rest of my family? How could I stop this feeling of being the black sheep of the family?

Luckily, I quit fighting myself and accepted my differences. Instead of fighting what my normal friends and media were telling me life should be like, I started to chase the crazy dreams of my youth.

What were the dreams of my youth? I imagined a life of adventure. *Indiana Jones, Swiss Family Robinson*, the cartoon *Talespin*. How could I make this a reality on $20,000 a year? Easy, I sold my truck, then I had no car payment, insurance, or gas expenses. I lived on a sailboat with no electricity or running water. I had the cheapest phone plan and was probably the last pilot in the world with a smartphone. I cut every possible corner when it came to saving money. I was passionate and determined to travel, I made it my priority, and I refused to let any excuses or fears stop me.

As a pilot, I was able to jumpseat all over the world for free. This allowed me to do short trips on my days off every month. I started my adventures by flying to the Out Islands of the Bahamas. I would walk out of the terminal, walk through the "bushes" until I found a secluded beach, and camp on some free piece of paradise. No tent, no hammock, just a tarp I had to roll myself up in when it rained. I read *Vagabonding* by Rolf Potts and learned how to travel cheap. I stayed in hostels that were one to ten dollars a night. I would only eat two meals a day. (I ate a lot of Ramen noodles.) I used local transportation, hitchhiked, or walked. I've slept with bums on the street, slept in a sleeping bag in a storage unit for a year, and slept on a guy's couch (in a nice beach condo) for $400 a month. I worked at a hostel while I was traveling.

The point is anything is possible. You have to figure out how to make it happen. It's not easy—you must sacrifice some comforts, but once you take that first leap, your confidence and imagination will grow exponentially. People still ask me when I am going to settle down and live a normal life. I never did find a normal life, but I found something so much better: I learned how to live an amazing life. Now I wonder, when is everyone else going to stop living a normal life?

HOW THIS BOOK CAN CHANGE YOUR LIFE

I went from smoking a pack of cigarettes a day, drinking every night, biting my fingernails, watching hours of useless videos when I was bored or even when I wasn't, procrastinating on writing a book for fifteen years, and consistently gaining twenty pounds at least once a year, to stopping all of this within three months.

This book will show you the formula I used to turn my life around. I am not promising that quitting your biggest addictions or overcoming your weaknesses will be easy. It will take some work on your part, but once you form a new life plan, you will be on your way to a better life.

I wrote this book while on my journey to fix myself. Did I find the magic words to fix everything? Nope. But I did realize no one can ever write the perfect book or create the perfect method to fix your life or mine. It's a continuous battle we must face daily. We conquer things in our lives and then new challenges arise.

This book is to help us face our daily struggles and accept our failures and difficulties in life as *challenges to overcome*. It will show you how to identify problems that need to be fixed or habits that you need to quit (like smoking) and "problems" that just need to be embraced or worked on (like being an introvert).

Above all, it shows you how to take control. We cannot accept our weaknesses as life being unfair. We must find the courage and the answers to rise above our addictions, bad habits, and the feelings of not being perfect. We must find the courage to shape the life we want.

I have (almost) always lived a life following my dreams and not someone else's. Not having a degree, never being in the corporate world, and never having a close group of friends who I frequently hung out with (because I was always traveling, not because I don't like my friends!) allowed me to form my own views on how to live my best life. My only nine-to-five job was moving furniture to get through flight school. I have bussed tables, was a bartender in Cambodia, and also had a newspaper route during flight school. Now I am a captain flying Boeing 747s around the world. I spent fifteen years of my life making well below the average income in the USA. I enjoyed every second of it. 2011 was one of the best years of traveling I've ever had, and I only made $15,000 that year! I have been fortunate to learn all the lessons from living paycheck to paycheck, realizing that money can't buy happiness. I've also been fortunate to realize mo' money doesn't necessarily mean mo' problems.

This book will help you no matter what your current life situation may be. If you are broke, in debt, lost, and without passion, I've been there. If you are doing well financially but feeling lost and without passion, I've been there too. Even if you think your life is 100 percent perfect right now, we can find a way to make life even better. You will gain freedom from yourself and your addictions. You will gain confidence. Whether you need a complete life makeover or just want to take your life to the next level, this book is for you. Kiss all your fears and misery goodbye. A new life awaits you.

So, why should you listen to me? I have no rags-to-riches story; I haven't overcome any disabilities or had any heartbreaking tragedy in my life. I don't have an impressive following on social media; I am not famous or recognized in any way at being an expert at what I am writing about. I got a C+ in high school English and never graduated from a university.

This is exactly why you should listen to me. I am probably a lot like you. I have struggled my whole life, wondering who I am, and why I think the way I do. I have struggled with many addictions. I had to learn to overcome them all without any super willpower or extra motivation.

This book is for average people (like me) who don't want to be average anymore. I'm not talking about becoming a billionaire or climbing to the top of the corporate ladder. All I want is for you to change your life from average to amazing. It's about accomplishing your wildest dreams and removing anything negative from your current lifestyle.

I want you to wake up every day and be excited to live.

RULES FOR SUCCESS

1. **Take notes.** If you want this book to work. If you are serious about changing your life. The only way my plan works is if you write things down. What will you need? Paper and something to write with. Napkin and crayon, back of a receipt, I don't care. I recommend a small journal or notebook you can keep with you all day. Write down any excuses you find yourself making. Write down any areas you want to fix or learn more about. And of course, write out your game plan for life—that is the whole point of this book. Throughout the book I will politely remind you in capital, bold letters of Rule #1. **WRITE IT DOWN!**
2. **Keep an open mind.** You must be willing to change and accept there may be a different or better way to do things. I'm not going to tell you how to live or the right way to live. That is for you to figure out. The right way to live is whatever is inside of you, beneath all the brainwashing. You must be willing to replace old habits, traditions, and knowledge with a new plan to jump-start your life. My best advice is to take no one's advice. Yes, even mine. Think for yourself.
3. **No excuses.** Pay attention to anytime you find yourself

making excuses for your life. Think about each topic. Is there a way you could get better? There is always a way. If you find yourself making an excuse, and you learn to say, "this will be difficult, but I can find a way," you win. Don't lie to yourself. Don't compare yourself to others. Whatever excuses you find yourself making, **WRITE IT DOWN**.
4. **You need to put in the effort.** Nothing is Free! Easy! Quick! Or Now! Everyone wants the free and quick way to get rich, lose weight, get an erection, or quit something. You are always promised the secret to something, but they never tell you what the secret is. I will tell you right now, for free! The secret is effort. Do not think reading this book, or any other book or online gimmick, will magically transform your life. Realize you must do the work. I *will not* tell you exactly what to eat or what exercises to do or what to invest in. I *will* help you set up a plan for winning life. I *will* help you to design a personal plan to elevate your life. Here's my top secret, free, quick, and easy formula to succeed in life:

(Hard Work + Dedication) × (Sacrifice + Effort) = Success

PART I

QUIT BAD HABITS AND ADDICTIONS

The history of my relationship with smoking. I started smoking because I thought it was what tough guys did. I hated smoking though, and it interfered with my bass fishing. So, I started chewing. Now I could be tough and fish at the same time, genius! It got to the point where I could tell dipping was negatively affecting my gums. I decided to take up smoking again (because I hated it and thought I couldn't get addicted) instead of chewing tobacco. Success! I haven't dipped in over fifteen years! Unfortunately, I became a pack-a-day smoker for fifteen years.

But there was a time when I quit for two whole years without one craving. It was amazing until that one day, ten years ago. I was having the worst day ever. Everything in my life sucked. I was in a crash pad (hotel room with a bunch of bunk beds for pilots), watching football and drinking beers with a couple of the guys, trying to unwind after the worst day ever. I don't think I would have smoked had it not been for a pack of cigarettes and lighter sitting right below the TV, staring at my subconscious mind the whole time. It wasn't until about beer six that my conscious mind even noticed them.

"Whose cigarettes?" I asked.

My friends shrugged. "Some guy left them. They're free."

Damn, free. If only I knew back then what I know now (nothing is free!). I spent the next ten years trying every possible method to quit. This book was born out of those ten years of research, trial and error, and a lot of soul searching.

Why we should quit our bad habits. If you change what you do when you are bored, stressed, need to concentrate, or relax, you will become infinitely more successful. What do you do when you are bored? Click through channels on the television? Eat? Smoke? Drink? What if instead you read a book on something that needs improvement in your life? What if you worked on a side business? What if you pursued something you are passionate about? The amount of time and money we waste can be alarming when we add it all up.

Everyone knows someone who is proud of being a functional alcoholic, drug user, smoker, gambler, overeater, or sex addict. But few of us like to refer to ourselves as addicts. So, let's not call anyone an addict. Just ask yourself, how many excuses are you making for your actions? Could your life be better if you broke your bad habit or addiction? I am not here to judge you. I want to make you aware of lies you have been telling yourself. If you find yourself making excuses, this is your evil little ego wanting you to continue to feed him his fix. Everyone has these thoughts; our goal is to become aware of them. **WRITE DOWN** the excuses that you find yourself making.

Why addictions are so hard to break. Either our bad habit contains an addictive substance like nicotine, or these addictions become our way to deal with discomfort in our lives. The irony is most bad habits are usually hard to form. You have to force yourself to like something. How many people actually enjoyed the taste of their first beer or shot? Can you remember how disgusting your first smoke was? Has anyone started a gambling addiction by winning one hundred times in a row? What about the first time you overate at an all-you-can-eat buffet and got sick? Or the guilt you feel for cheating on your spouse?

The good news is we can also become conditioned to the taste of plain vegetables, black coffee, egg whites, breathing air instead of smoke, enjoying water, and a clear mind. Ask yourself if you are really drinking that tequila because you love the taste. Or is it for a different reason?

Why good habits are so hard to maintain. How many people got out of the habit of going to the gym during COVID-19 when every gym in the world was closed? I am guilty of that. We easily fall out of good habits, because we want to be comfortable. The world has become extremely comfortable. Most people in the USA are only a click away on their phone from relieving some minor annoyance that everyone in the world experiences daily. Too hot in the room? Click, air conditioner goes down two degrees. Bored? Click, video of talking-dog-dressed-like-cowboy reaction video (SHOCKED). Hungry? Click, fast food is on the way. Your nose is runny, click, you definitely have COVID-19.

I'm not against smartphones. For every time-wasting app, there are useful ones as well. The point is we always want to be comfortable, and this is what leads us to fall out of good habits.

Why we continue to do things we regret but have such a hard time doing things that give us satisfaction. It's in our human programming. We want to eat when we are hungry, we want something to do when we are bored to relieve the boredom. We get lonely because we are programmed to want to reproduce. Why is it so much easier to drink beer and watch television after a long day than go to the gym? Because it is easy. Because it is more comfortable.

Although at first going to the gym seems tough, after a while it becomes a habit. Instead of a hangover in the morning, you have energy that spills over to everything in your life. Have you ever gone to the gym and said, "I wish I wouldn't have gone to the gym?" No. Have you ever eaten a healthy meal that satisfied your hunger and said, "I wish I would have eaten fast food instead?" No. Have you ever woken up from a hangover and said, "Why did I drink so much last night?" Always. **The satisfaction of getting things done needs to become your reward.** Quit rewarding your evil little ego with bad habits that do not benefit your life.

Bad habits—Difficult to form. Difficult to quit.

Good habits—Easy to form. Easy to break.

If you take anything from this book, let it be the above quote. Think about this throughout the book. This is the conclusion I have formed after reading numerous self-help books about quitting bad habits and/or starting good habits that didn't help me. Why didn't any of those books work for me? Because they failed to mention this simple equation. You can easily form a habit in whatever number of days the latest study shows; however, those habits can be broken even more easily in a couple days! This book will show you how you can keep your good habits alive and get rid of your bad habits.

Since we already formed our bad habits, let's figure out how to quit them. In Part II, we will learn how to create a quality lifestyle (good habits) and maintain them.

THREE TYPES OF BAD HABITS

Habits you can block or stay away from. Not too many habits fall into this category, but you are lucky if they do. If you self-exclude yourself from casinos or websites, you can't gamble. If you can block pornography from all devices, you can't watch it. I guarantee you could quit watching hours of television if you give your TV away. If you set your phone to only allow an hour of internet time per day, then you will not look like a crackhead swiping at your phone all day. If you shaved your head, you would not be able to twirl your hair.

Try this method of blocking first (not shaving your head, that was a joke), even if the bad habit is not something you can permanently block. For example, not keeping fattening foods in your house. But if you can't block it or make it invisible, move on to the next type of habit.

Habits you can quit now. Within a week of living with a girl for the first time, I formed a new habit of putting the toilet seat down. It was easy, I just had to be aware of when I was doing it and stop. Leaving the toilet seat up ceased being a habit.

We all have a lot of bad habits we do without even thinking about them. Start becoming aware of what you do. Do you pace around every time you are on the phone? Do you roll your eyes at people? Do you get angry easily? Do you bite your fingernails? Becoming more aware can solve a lot of these kinds of habits.

When you buy a new phone, you must reprogram your mind to learn which button takes a picture. While writing this book, I quit putting two spaces after a period. Why are these habits so easy to break when other habits are not? Because every time you push a button, and the camera turns off instead of taking a picture, you eventually change the habit. Every time I typed two spaces after a period, a little blue line showed up, telling me I was doing something wrong.

So, habits you can quit now can be easily fixed by becoming aware of when you are doing them, or by having some type of action to tell you to change. If you can hire someone to punch you in the face every time you gamble, eat a donut, or smoke, you could probably quit without difficulty. I remember joking with my friends, telling them they had my permission to kick me in the nuts if they ever saw me smoking. Since we may enjoy how our face looks or may want kids in the future, let's look at other options to quit our most difficult habits to break.

The Beast: your most difficult habit to break. This category of bad habits is sneaky. Smoking one cigarette does no harm to you immediately. When you eat a cookie, you don't immediately see your gut or butt increase in size. There is no electric shock when you place a bet. The reason these habits are difficult to break is because there is no immediate action that tells us we are doing something wrong (once we force ourselves to become conditioned to the action). Instead, we get a dopamine hit that temporarily rewards our evil little ego.

How many times have you tried to quit and failed? I tried everything to quit smoking: dozens of books, podcasts, willpower, substitutes (mints, gum, pouches, patches), smoking one less every day, imagining I had an iguana that lived on my shoulder and would talk me out of smoking (not my idea, read it in a book), and even making myself puke when I craved a cigarette (another book).

Part I of this book is going to primarily deal with this third category of bad habits: The Beast (a.k.a. your most difficult habit to break). Through the next sections, I'm going to talk you through some of the theory and practices behind habit breaking—and then tie it together, so you can implement it today.

THE PROCESS OF QUITTING

Why can some people seem to be able to quit a bad habit cold turkey, while others find it the most difficult thing in the world? Easy, either they are liars, forgetful, or were never addicted.

Do not be discouraged by others who have seemingly quit something so easily, and you cannot.

There is always some other reason someone can quit cold turkey. Either they physically cannot handle the cigarette, do not have a sweet tooth, get no high from gambling, or they simply have no interest in any other bad habit. They may have a fear of being judged by others, or God. They may fear for their health. They could also have a positive reason to quit, such as having their first kid or wanting to attract a significant other. There is always some motivation to quit.

In other words, people are generally able to walk away from bad habits or an addiction due to three reasons: motivation, fear, or no desire to continue the habit. I was able to quit smoking the first time I tried because I had motivation. I wanted to impress a girl. Other people are able to walk away from vices because of religion. Either out of faith or fear, usually a combination of both, some religious people can find ways to get through life. Still others can quit because they lose interest in the habit.

The second time I tried to quit, I had no motivation, fear, or real desire to quit—which made quitting nearly impossible. The key to succeeding, I realized, is to access that third category, i.e., no desire to continue the habit. This book will focus on the addictions you want to quit but can't find the motivation or fear to quit. It will help you to remove the desire to continue doing the habit you want to quit.

We all know that our addictions are bad for us. We know we are negatively affecting our lives by continuing our addiction, so why can't we stop? It's because our evil little ego wants to be happy all the time.

Your crutch always gets the credit for "fixing" your problem and making you feel temporarily better. But your crutch IS the problem!

So how do we stop that evil little ego from tricking us into thinking that something we really don't want to do will make us feel better? We must distract it. If you have tried to quit before and it hasn't worked out, we need to go on a mission to find out why. First, let's figure out what you want to quit or cut back on in your life.

IDENTIFY YOUR PROBLEM

Do not look up the definition of an alcoholic or addiction online to find out if you have a problem. Be honest with yourself. Are you addicted to something? Is there something or someone in your life you want to give up that you cannot? Yes, it is possible to be addicted to a person. It is also possible to be addicted to something that is accepted socially as a good thing, such as having a perfect body, reading self-help books, or watching "educational" videos on television or the internet. I literally have to remind myself to read a Doc Ford novel every once in a while and just chill.

Think you are not addicted to something? Fine, then try to give it up for a week.

Why do we make excuses for our bad habits and addictions? Because we are afraid to give them up. Either we have failed quitting before, or we have some deeper issues we don't think we can face without our crutch. We drink, smoke, eat, or whatever, to hide from a feeling, emotion, or past experience we are afraid or ashamed of. But this is normal, everyone has things in their life that we try to hide from others or even ourselves.

We don't always do these habits when trying to suppress feelings or emotions. Sometimes, it's just fun to drink with your buddies during the game. Or we may smoke socially with friends while we are having a good time. You overeat at Christmas because you are with loved ones, and the food is plentiful. But when we try to quit, and we can't, this is what we must change in our lives.

If you have the desire to quit, but continue to fail, then there is a bigger issue in your life you must figure out.

Here's how you can go about identifying if you have a problem.

Find out where you are wasting time and money. How many hours do you spend on your phone, computer, TV, or video games? Time it. Set a timer and figure out how much time you are wasting. How much time and money do you waste smoking, drinking, or gambling? How many hours do you spend on worthless busy work, emails, swiping on your phone, or watching television? How many hours procrastinating, complaining, being angry, or worrying? Time it and **WRITE IT DOWN**.

What made me quit smoking and drinking was I realized I wanted my time and freedom back:

- I smoked twenty cigarettes a day, multiplied by four minutes each, equals one hour and twenty minutes. Add in the time it takes to find a place to smoke, easily two hours a day.
- Three hundred days spent smoking over the next ten years. Almost a whole year of my life was wasted smoking!

- When I would smoke, I would want a drink. When I would drink, I wanted a smoke. It was a vicious cycle of wasting time, money, and health.
- A minimum of $20,000 on cigarettes alone over the next ten years. The money didn't bother me, I didn't see it as $20,000. It's only five to ten bucks here and there. What made me want to finally quit was to regain the freedom to live life without having to plan my day around the cigarette.
- Drinking didn't just waste an hour here or an hour there. It literally wasted my whole night. **Drinking was an excuse to be lazy.**

How do you want to improve your life? Over half of my life, I had many habits that were wasting my time and money. And the sad part was, I was happy for most of those years. That's what the ego does to us; it lies and tells us we are living a great life. Through social media, Hollywood, and music, our ego is reinforced that we are living the best life.

You can live a comfortable life following what you see others doing, indulging in the same habits as them, or trying to be like someone on television. Or, you can create a plan that will allow you to live *your* best life imaginable.

Once again, I'm not judging anyone on how they want to live their life. If you want a comfortable life, I have no problem and will not try to change you. This book is for people who want to take their life to the next level. I'm not talking about going from poverty to being a millionaire in a day. This is reality. **WRITE DOWN** what you want to quit or cut back on in life.

Write it down right now. Once you've got a list of what you waste time and money on, and thus what you want to quit in life, pause. Take a break. Come back to the book in five minutes after writing. Or sleep on it. But set a time for tomorrow to continue reading.

Don't stop now, don't let the fear that you are about to give up all your addictions creep in. This is your evil little ego coming in to say, *Screw this guy, he doesn't know what he is talking about.* It is more fun to go smoke or drink or eat. Don't give in to the fear. Having this fear is the first sign that you are ready to give up your addiction. Go have a smoke or drink or gamble or whatever. But ask yourself if it is permanently relieving any stress or actually making your life better.

FIND YOUR TRIGGERS

So now that you have identified the things you want to improve on, let's find out why you do these things.

Start paying attention anytime you are triggered to do your bad habit. You need to immediately write down every time you have a feeling of discomfort and want your fix. You don't have to quit right now. Simply **WRITE IT DOWN**.

This was a huge part in helping me quit my bad habits and addictions. You need to write down what happened to trigger you and also how you were feeling. Was it anger, depression, anxiety, did it feel like hunger, was something just not right? Or was it out of habit? Or was it so bad you felt like you might die if you didn't have a cookie or a smoke? That's how I felt. I wasn't scared of dying in the future. Sometimes I felt as if I might die immediately if I did not have a smoke. This is what your evil little ego tricks you into believing.

Make a list of all the times you break down or even crave your habit (i.e., your triggers). Then create a *contingency plan* for times when you have these cravings. Keep this list on you in paper form, put it on your phone; make it available anytime, anywhere, so you can look at it for strength.

This is a short list of some of the triggers (threats) I had, and examples of what I did to fight the craving (contingency plan). Do you share any of the same triggers I had for smoking?

THREAT	CONTINGENCY PLAN
When I woke up.	Make tea or coffee.
With coffee.	Just enjoy the damn coffee.
Anytime I did anything on my phone.	Put a picture of Will Ferrell licking a white dog turd on my background.
While driving, especially when stuck in traffic.	Keep a clean truck, no smoking in the truck.
When I was bored.	Read, meditate, study, gym, walk, run, ten push-ups, watch talking dog videos, hell, anything.
When the unexpected came up or plans changed.	Embrace the suffering. Deep breaths. Everything will pass.
After a long, hard, stressful, or even an easy day at work.	Run, yoga, read, gym, meditate, sleep…anything.
Having feelings of restlessness.	Embrace the suffering, do something active.
Having the worst day ever.	Scream in a pillow, shadow box, hiss like an angry cat at anyone who looks at you. I hate days like these!
When drinking.	Do not drink when trying to quit.
Seeing or hearing someone else light up.	Know they really wish they were a nonsmoker like you. They are not solving anything.
Before work.	Enjoy not having to go outside for a smoke. Get MGFD accomplished (see Part III).

THREAT	CONTINGENCY PLAN
After taking a crap.	Wash my hands and enjoy them not smelling like smoke (or poop).
After the first cigarette didn't fix my problem (chain-smoke).	Do you really think the second one will?
During or after a meal.	Now you can actually enjoy the meal! Keep mints around the first few weeks.
An annoying text message or email.	Deep breaths, it's only a message.
Being reminded of some stressful thing you have to do. (Like taking out the trash.)	Just take out the damn trash!
Sometimes it hits you out of nowhere.	This is the hardest because it's unexpected. This is where I pull out my contingency plan and find something on the list to do.
When the sun set. (This is because the sun going down usually signifies parties starting and drinking.)	Enjoy the sunset, know the sun will come back up. Have an evening routine planned out.
When I was hungry.	Eat! Keep healthy snacks like almonds handy.
When I was tired.	Sleep! Read something that puts you to sleep.

So anything that happened to me, good or bad, I needed to smoke afterwards. Trying to avoid certain situations could not fix my problem (you can't hold a poop in forever). Smoking was my Beast, and this contingency plan formed a part of the bigger plan that would eventually save me.

Other things I used to combat triggers: taking a big whiff of Tiger Balm, sugar-free mints and gum, going to the mirror and giving myself a pep talk, start laughing to myself like a crazy person (note to self: don't do this in the cockpit anymore), or whatever the situation called for. I think the best option is to do something active. Get some fresh air if you can, or start doing jumping jacks or push-ups until it passes.

Triggers are important to recognize before anything else. Start realizing every time you feel like you are wanting to give in to your bad habits. This will also help you when you quit, and you have a trigger come out of nowhere. You will know that these feelings will creep back in the future, but you will be prepared, and over time you will learn to completely ignore them.

In most situations, it was easy to acknowledge I was having a craving and move on. The most common times when I struggled were in the evening. I had to plan out every single minute of what I would do until it was time to go to bed just to avoid giving in to the trigger.

The hardest times will be when you have a combination of triggers happen at once. For example, tired after a long day at work, least favorite hotel, depressing weather, and having twenty emails pop up when you land after a sixteen-hour flight reminding you of all the crap you have to do. When all these pile on top of each other, you will need a good plan to fight the craving.

Some triggers will come out of nowhere, even years later. A certain place or event that happens, or something really unfortunate happens in your life, and your evil little ego tells you that you need something a little extra to make the pain go away.

Unlike what you will read in almost any other book or study about quitting addictions, I believe there is no set number of days you need to quit something for it to cease being a problem. Don't think you are invincible after three days, two weeks, or even two years after you have quit. You need a game plan to be prepared for the rest of your life. I wish I had a game plan on that dreary night in the crash pad ten years ago!

IDENTIFY THE EXCUSES YOU ARE MAKING

What is holding you back from changing your ways? I will make an educated guess. Fear. We are all afraid to give up our little crutch, whether it's ice cream, cigarettes, alcohol, drugs, sex, television, or swiping at your phone like a crackhead. And so we make excuses.

Making excuses never solved any problem. We all make excuses to justify not living up to our potential. Excuses can go hand in hand with your triggers:

- I had a hard day; I deserve a cigarette.
- My life is so unfair; I deserve to be depressed and eat a gallon of ice cream.

Or they can be old beliefs you hold on to:

- Can't teach an old dog new tricks.
- I love food too much to be skinny.

- I used to work out until I had kids; now, I'm too busy.
- If I had kids, I would probably quit smoking.
- I like my Dad bod.

Once again, I'm not judging anyone. If you are truly happy with your body or your habit, then I have no problem with that. This book is for people who don't want to settle for a comfortable life anymore. This is for people who want to be their best and are not 100 percent satisfied with themselves right now.

Remember, no one really cares what you do. Don't let people tell you "it's easy for you because…" or "you are lucky because…" It's all excuses for their ego to feel better. People always tell me I'm lucky that I am skinny. They say, "Wait until you turn ____ years old." It's funny—when I was in my twenties, it was wait until I turn thirty. Now it is wait until I turn forty. Or maybe I'm skinny because I eat healthy and work out? There were many times in my life when I gained up to twenty pounds seemingly overnight. I do not have a perfect metabolism, nor do I have ridiculous skinny genes. I prefer bellbottoms.

What excuses did I use to tell myself?

"**I have an addictive personality.**" I choose not to believe this statement. Who cares if it may or may not run in my family. The more I believed it, the more I was doomed to be an addictive person. It made it that much harder to quit. Now I use my same old excuse, but with reverse psychology on my own brain (is that possible?). I flipped it around and chose to become addicted to living an amazingly productive and healthy life.

"**I like smoking.**" Lies, all lies! I told myself this because smoking didn't hurt me. I could smoke a pack or two a night and wake up feeling normal with no nasty cough or any other negative side effects. But when I truly was honest with myself, I didn't really like smoking. If someone would have offered me a pill that was guaranteed to cure my addiction forever (with no side effects), I would have taken it without thinking twice.

"You can't be all good, you have to balance it out." I would use this excuse at the grocery store when I would buy a pack of cigarettes and a six-pack on the way back from a run or from the gym. The cashiers almost always made a comment about buying cigarettes after a workout. Nobody likes a Goody Two-Shoes, but it's also okay to not feel guilty about being healthy.

Here are some of the more common excuses I hear from other people.

"Life is unfair." Everyone in the world has issues. I like to refer to them as challenges from God, the universe, or unicorns. Your life is not worse than anyone else's. Life is not unfair. If you think your life is unfair, do a bit of traveling. You have to change yourself from the inside. Realize it is no one's fault but your own. It doesn't run in your family, and you don't continue your addiction because of any other excuse except the excuses your evil little ego is making.

"It's not comfortable." You don't like to do it? Most people don't like going to the gym. I am rarely motivated to go. Yoga is extremely difficult and uncomfortable for me. I hate stretching. I am not really interested in stocks or crypto. I don't enjoy doing my budget. I don't like to brush my teeth. I hate cold showers.

Why do I do all these things? Because afterwards I always feel better. It is the opposite of doing things that are comfortable. Do you really feel better after a cigarette, after drinking, after overeating, losing all your money, swiping at your phone, or buying things you don't need online? No, you feel better while you are doing it, but when you stop, your evil little ego wants more. It will never be satisfied.

"I'm too lazy to quit." I hear this excuse all the time. Usually the person says it in a joking way and everyone laughs…but it's not funny! It's sad that as a society, we have come to associate being lazy as cool, cute, or funny. If you label yourself as lazy, you are justifying to yourself that it is okay to be lazy. But you are only setting yourself up to live a life well below your true potential. Lying around all day with your partner sounds romantic, and it can be, just don't make it a habit. We all think we are lazy because we like to be comfortable. But being lazy will get you nowhere, will not gain you respect with others (even if they laugh), and will not be attractive to a quality partner.

"I live for the moment." This is such a stupid thing people say: *you have to live for the moment!* No, this encourages every bad habit. Living for the moment is something our bad ego uses to give us an excuse to do things we will regret. YOLO (you only live once) does not mean you should party every night or eat foods that taste good every meal.

"At least I'm not a crackhead." It is easy to look at other people's addictions or bad habits and justify our own addictions as not being as bad. This falls under Rule #3, don't compare yourself to others. It's like being addicted to cocaine and saying, "Well, at least I'm not a crackhead."

"**Uncle Frank was a smoker.**" We all know or heard of someone whose diet was bacon, beer, and cigarettes, and who lived to be 103. Do you think it's a good idea to smoke and eat bacon every day? Of course not. That person is very rare, just like finding your soulmate when you are sixteen is very rare. Don't wait around sulking because your life has not played out like a romantic comedy. Put in the work, make yourself better, and get busy living. Only one in a billion people (I made this stat up) die from walking in front of a bus. Would you walk in front of a bus because you like your chances?

What excuses are you making for your addiction? **WRITE DOWN** all the excuses you are making for yourself. Could you flip an excuse you previously used? For example: you only live once, so I better stop smoking, so I don't end up like Uncle Fred who died at age fifty from lung cancer.

MAKE A PROS AND CONS LIST

This is one of the most important stages. You have to think of every reason why you continue to do your bad habit. Are there any advantages at all? Maybe you are doing it for a deeper reason than simply being addicted. Hopefully, if you are honest with yourself, the negative effects from your habit will heavily outweigh the positives.

If you find yourself having pros for your bad habit, take a hard look at why you think that is a positive advantage. For example, smokers always say they like smoking because other smokers are nice people and are interesting to talk to while smoking. Fine, then just go down and talk to the smokers without smoking! Ask yourself if your evil little ego is making an excuse and is giving your crutch undue credit. I still think smokers are enjoyable to talk to, I just realized they are just as pleasant to talk to without having to smoke!

Take a sheet of paper and split it into two sections (much like what you did with triggers and contingency plans). On one side, **WRITE DOWN** how much better your life could be without this addiction (pros). On the other side, **WRITE DOWN** any negatives you can think of from quitting this habit (cons).

Usually, the list of pros will far outweigh any cons you can think of. Here is an example of some of my pros and cons for quitting smoking.

PROS FOR QUITTING	CONS
I will not stink.	There are zero negative reasons for quitting.
It is messy (ashes, cigarette burns, etc.).	
I will not feel guilty buying cigarettes or lighting up around other people.	
I will gain confidence, energy, self-esteem, and my freedom.	
I will not have to plan my day around the cigarette.	
I will not feel jittery or have the feeling that something is missing every twenty minutes.	
It does not cure stress, boredom, anxiety, or depression.	
I will enjoy my meals more.	
Smoking leads to drinking, drinking leads to being lazy.	
Does not help me concentrate. You can't type with a cigarette in your hand!	
The cigarette gets the credit for making me feel better, but the cigarette is the problem!	
I will have more time, money, health, and be attractive to my future wife. Would I want her to be a smoker? Hell no! Gross!	

As you can see, the pros far outweigh the cons. Even if the bad habit is small (such as biting your nails), and you do not have a huge list of pros, think of the confidence you will gain by conquering your nail-biting habit.

Have an attitude of victory. I'm not just quitting something, I am destroying The Beast. If I never feed The Beast, it will die. Where is the desire to continue smoking? Smoking has no real benefits—it's all an illusion that the cigarette gets credit for. Same with caffeine, alcohol, food, drugs, and gambling. There is no benefit. There is only a small pleasure we get that temporarily gives us the illusion of feeling better. But if this solved anything, then why would we need another smoke, drink, cookie, hit, pull, drag, swipe, click, or bet? Would you eat a dog turd? No, you have no desire to do that. You wouldn't eat it because it stinks and comes out of a dog's butt. Cigarettes are a lot dirtier than a dog's butt. We have to force ourselves into liking bad things, and now we have to learn how to stop.

KEEP TRACK OF YOUR FAILURES

The key to success in this book is to **WRITE DOWN** and keep track of your triggers and your failures. Write down every time you have the urge to do your habit. Write it down the moment you find yourself having a thought about your addiction. Write down what you could do to distract yourself. What could you do instead of giving in to your evil little ego? Anytime you have an urge, **WRITE DOWN** *WHY*. This is important because it will help you realize that most of the time you are triggered, there probably is a pattern or common theme. Maybe it is during a certain time of day or after something happens, maybe it is just your body telling you it needs something (like food or sleep), but you mistake that feeling as needing your crutch.

More importantly, anytime you fail to shake the urge, **WRITE DOWN** *WHY* you failed, and how you felt before and after. Was it worth giving in to your urge, or did you feel worse about yourself afterwards? Did your crutch really fix anything? This is the most important thing. **WRITE IT DOWN.** Don't just think about it.

You need to keep track of all the reasons you may fail, or why you failed. Only then can you learn from it. You must retrain your brain into knowing that giving in will not help anything. The brain is quick to forget thanks to our evil little ego. Writing down every time I failed helped me to realize over time, my crutch never fixed anything. It only made me feel worse. The original condition was still there (hunger, boredom, stress, anxiety, tiredness, etc.) plus I felt worse by giving in!

Keep in mind that everyone fails sometimes—progress is not a linear path. When you fail, accept your failure, **write it down**, and learn from it. Consider it one step closer to killing The Beast!

LAST THOUGHTS ON QUITTING

Willpower and motivation. Online, you will find most websites mention the best way to quit an addiction is with willpower and motivation. This is where I come in and tell you the actual way to quit bad habits. You will never suddenly become motivated and stay that way the rest of your life. No one has enough willpower to stop their biggest problem alone. You cannot block all temptation. You cannot create a perfect schedule. Life is unpredictable. What you need is a new lifestyle. You cannot just change a couple habits. You need something you will live by for the rest of your life.

Everyone thinks they have to get really motivated to do something. There is no motivation pill. Motivational books are great, for a couple days, maybe a month. I love motivational books, but it's kind of like reading the same advice over and over again. You have to create a life with good habits so that on days when you are not motivated, your routine kicks in, and you still get things done.

Self-induced motivation breeds unconscious motivation.

The more we force ourselves into doing what we know is best for us, even though we do not want to do it, the better our chances that the action will become a habit. You will never wake up every day with an unlimited source of motivation. It's a constant process.

Timing. Every addiction needs to be treated differently. For some addictions, the best timing is now. In everyone's life, there will be times that are so stressful that the last thing you could possibly do would be to defeat The Beast. It also could be the best time. Say you have a baby on the way. Exciting but also stressful, however, you have a really good reason to quit. I don't believe setting a date is a good way to solve anything. I used to tell myself I would wait until I had no stress in my life to quit smoking. I thought, "Well when this happens, I'll be ready to quit smoking." Ten years, seventy thousand cigarettes, and $20,000 later, I was still wanting to quit every day. Ten years ago, I was making $30,000 a year! Almost a whole extra year of work spent just on cigarettes! Never use the excuse that you will wait until the timing is right. That will NEVER happen!

Quit when you are ready. Do not try to pick the perfect moment, or to quit on some special occasion. Here is a short list of some of the interesting places where I have "quit" smoking:

- Cape of Good Hope, South Africa
- From the top of Temple IV, Tikal, Guatemala
- Who knew you could buy cigarettes in the Darien Gap?
- Baladin Beach Hotel, Pingwe, Zanzibar (my favorite hotel in the world)
- On a cargo boat down the Amazon River

There will never be a perfect time to quit. You have to start quitting now. Go through all the failures, find out every trigger. Do not set a date. Unless this has worked for you in the past, quit when you are ready. Setting a date to quit only causes stress, which usually leads to wanting to do your bad habit more to relieve stress.

Do not think by waiting until you remove some other cause of stress in your life that it will be easier to quit. For example, when I finally had a job that paid good money, and I finally got out of debt and had no stress in my life due to money, it became harder to quit certain things. Now spending money on cigarettes, food, and alcohol ceased to be a thought. It was much easier to justify the bad habits because they weren't breaking the bank. Keeping a budget even when you have plenty of money is always a good idea to help you realize how much money you spend on certain things.

Realize your ego wants pleasure now. When all you want is a feeling of pleasure, your rational ego needs to step in. We must learn to deal with temporary uncomfortable feelings. We all deal with these slight feelings of discomfort differently, and most of us are unaware of what we are doing when we are not in a harmonious state.

Your ego wants to be happy all the time, wants to do fun things that make you feel good with as little effort as possible. You have to step in and learn to deal with temporary uncomfortable feelings that everyone has on a day-to-day basis. Your life will start to change exponentially if you can learn to start living without your crutches. You don't need to suppress a slightly negative feeling to survive.

If you are having feelings that life is not right at the moment, and you think sucking on a stick and blowing smoke will solve anything, you are crazy. You think a cookie or bag of chips is going to add joy to your life? You think you won't have the same damn craving and slightly uncomfortable feeling in thirty minutes? You had a hard day, so you reward yourself with alcohol? This is stupid, you are setting yourself up to feel horrible the next day as well. You buy that new thing for your house that will make it perfect, then next week you find something better that goes in that spot, and the cycle continues. Do you gamble and dream of becoming rich overnight? Whether it's sports or lotto, it's a waste.

Know that these uncomfortable feelings are the body telling you something is wrong. You are hungry, or tired, or angry, and you need to calm TF down. Every day you will have these slight uncomfortable feelings. You need to start to embrace the suffering. Suffering is a big, scary word. But life is full of suffering. We will never be 100 percent happy all the time.

Combine your problems. This may seem like you are trying to stop too many bad things at once. The more bad habits you can quit at one time, the easier it will be. For example, if you quit smoking and drinking, you might have a harder time going to sleep, but by working out and going for a walk you become tired, and by meditating you become less stressed. You will also want to eat better when you exercise, and if you exercise, it will make you want to eat healthier. It becomes one big hap-hap-happy cycle.

Get rid of negative influences. Move, break up, quit your job. The hardest step is the first. Have you ever rappelled down a cliff? I highly recommend it. The first step backward is terrifying. After that you wonder why you did not do this a long time ago and are amazed how easy and fun it is. The next time you go, the first step is still scary, but it is a hell of a lot easier. It is the same with leaving something you are used to.

Are there people in your life who are holding you back, but you don't want to let them down? By letting yourself down, you are letting the entire world down. If you tell your drinking or gambling (or insert your addiction here) buddies you are going to stop drinking or gambling, and they *don't* give you crap and call you names, they are probably not really your friends. If you tell them you are really serious about this, and they *still* give you crap, they are probably not really your friends. Get rid of them. If you happen to have great friends, then use them as accountability partners to help you.

Read as many books as possible about your problem. I like reading books written by someone who was also addicted to the same problem. Don't stop trying to quit. Read all sixty thousand self-help books on Kindle if you have to. There is a way for all of us, we just have to find it.

Change location. This book started out (fifteen years ago) as a book about how traveling can solve all your problems. This is the whole "take the first step backward off the cliff" metaphor. It will be scary and seem impossible, but you may have to remove yourself from a circumstance you are in altogether.

Do not use bad substitutes. Trust me. Quit all of it. Don't quit gambling by playing Candy Crush. Don't quit coffee by drinking Coke. Don't quit a sex addiction with pornography. And for the love of someone, don't try to quit chewing tobacco by smoking! You have a nicotine addiction more than a smoking addiction. Until you have tried all other methods, do not try to solve any problems with prescribed pills. (But of course, consult someone who has a degree, unlike myself, first.) You need to realize you don't always need something or need to be doing something. Mindfulness and meditation are a huge help with this, and we talk about it in Part II.

You will need substitutes, but we talk about that in Part II as well. You will need to substitute your old bad habits with new good habits.

FORM YOUR GAME PLAN TO QUIT

Your game plan to quit is as simple as writing everything down, and keeping the plan with you. **WRITE DOWN** your list of triggers and your contingency plan. **WRITE DOWN** your list of pros and cons. You must **WRITE DOWN** every time you fail. If you don't, your evil little ego will surprisingly forget the way you felt when you failed. Why would you relapse when it makes you feel worse about yourself? You want your crutch to feel better, but it doesn't make anything better! Every time I went from not smoking without a problem for a few days to breaking down and lighting up, I hated it more every single time. This is the key. Do not stop quitting. Quit every damn day if you have to. The humiliation and weakness I felt after giving in was eventually enough motivation to quit for good.

We will never be perfect tomorrow. We will never be perfect. But if we get a little better each day, if we have more positive days than negative, then we are getting better. That is all we can do, try. Never give up. The winner never quits quitting.

If you have the feeling of "that's all"? Just try it. Write it all down.

Quit. Fail. Quit. Fail. A million times if you have to, until you quit for good. If you don't see this method working, read other books. Everyone will have their own method to quit. Maybe the talking reptile on your shoulder will work for you? But this is not all, the other key is to distract the evil little ego. We can do this by forming a new way of living. By changing our whole lives and filling up our day with productive, beneficial activities, the desire to waste our time on something that is hurting us will fade away.

Next, we find out how to supercharge our lives by exchanging bad habits with a new life routine.

THE GET BUSY LIVING PLAN TO QUIT: RECAP

Identify your problems. **Write them down.**

Identify how much time and/or money you are wasting. **Write it down.**

Identify your triggers. Create a contingency plan for your triggers. **Write them down.**

Figure out what excuses you are making. **Write them down.**

Pros and cons. **Write them down.**

Keep track of your failures. **Write them down.**

Form your game plan. **Write it down.**

PART II

CREATE A QUALITY LIFESTYLE

How do you know when you are happy?

- In shape?
- Rich?
- Successful?
- A better person?
- A better parent?

The answer, you won't. We don't need one broad goal or New Year's resolution in our life. What we need is an entire lifestyle that supports a healthy, happy, successful life. A lifestyle we can live that keeps growing. If you set a goal to lose fifty pounds in six months, are you successful and fit if you achieve it? Maybe, but how long will it last? Do you really want to stay on your torture diet and exercise plan that costs a fortune forever?

A lot of books mention SMART goals. I think SMART goals are stupid. The goals look great on paper, but it is too difficult or unrealistic to keep a SMART goal forever. It may help you lose fifty pounds, but it will not keep you from gaining them back.

We need to set simple routines we can complete every day in a short amount of time. Eventually these routines may turn into habits. From there we can build on the habits. But remember my formula from earlier?

Bad habits—Difficult to form. Difficult to quit.

Good habits—Easy to form. Easy to break.

So, we eventually have to figure out a way to avoid breaking those good habits.

To start out, let's look at the areas in your life that you might want to improve. Can you think of new routines you could introduce to better these areas? The key is to look at each part of your life and see where making a change in one category can benefit the rest. It may sound contradictory to other advice you have heard, but I believe it is easier to get your whole life together all at once than take it one step at a time.

INTRODUCING FRANKLIN PATRICK MESSY

F.P. Messy. This is the acronym I use to check in on my life. Financial, Physical, Mental, Emotional, Spiritual, Social, and You (Your Passions). I remember it using F.P. Messy. As in the famous psychologist, Franklin Patrick Messy. Okay I made that guy up. This is a stupid acronym, but just remember it somehow, okay? Fat Phat Messy?

You might look at my list of ways to improve your F.P. Messy and say, "I already knew all that." Agreed, most of the advice below is well known; however, a lot of the advice I did not know anything about or was not practicing until very recently. Ask yourself if you are *actually* living what you already *know*.

Get out a piece of paper and write each letter down the side.

F
P
M
E
S
S
Y

Before you read any further, **WRITE DOWN** anything you can think of that you would want to improve in each category. If you can't think of anything, read some of the suggestions in the sections below, where we look at each category in detail. The following is only a short list of potential advice. It is up to you to figure out small goals you could do to improve your life. There are sixty thousand self-help books on Kindle alone. If you want more info about a particular section, read about it.

FINANCIAL

Make and follow a budget. The most important thing to do, whether you are living paycheck to paycheck, or if you are financially free. Know where your money is going. When was the last time you did your budget? There are plenty of good apps out there to help you track your budget as well as see which categories you are spending the most amount of money on.

Get out of debt. Stay out of debt. If this is where you are, stick with the basics. Find ways to get rid of your debt as quickly as possible. Always pay above the minimum payment when you are paying off anything with interest (credit card, loan). Figure out how much money you would save in interest by paying your debt off early.

Live life below your means. When you get a pay raise, do not buy a new car or house. Live the same lifestyle with only a slight increase in quality of life, pay off debt, or invest the rest. Upgrade from the thrift store to the outlet mall, not designer clothes. Ramen noodles to something healthier, not eating out at fancy restaurants every night. Just because you make a lot of money does not mean you have to spend a lot of money. If you do not make a lot of money, don't try to pretend that you do.

Do not keep up with the Joneses. Everyone knows this. No one follows it! It is probably the most broken commandment in the Bible. Are you guilty of this? Maybe right now, you are not, but this is the reason we need to revisit these questions monthly, at least yearly, to keep track of our mischievous ego. Don't live a boring life, this book is about living it up. But keep this in mind when buying things you don't really need. For me, I have no problem paying a little extra for a cool experience. I get to keep that experience forever. If it has always been your dream to own a Ferrari, and you have the cash, get one. If you realized yesterday that your new dream is to drive a Ferrari, don't get one. Learn to just appreciate nice things without having them. Or rent them and see if it is something you really would want to take care of and pay for storage or maintenance. Airbnb a castle instead of buying one.

Only buy things you can pay for in cash. I'm not saying credit cards are bad. It is good to build credit, and most cards have perks such as hotel points, airline miles, cash back, etc. The problem with credit cards is they allow us to impulse buy. Nothing in life is so important that you need it now. Make a rule to never buy anything on a credit card immediately. Give yourself two days to think if that item would benefit your life, or is the purchase just to satisfy the evil little ego?

Set up autopay to pay your full balance every month.

Think about your retirement. No matter what age you are. Do a quick online retirement calculator, or search "how much money do I need to retire." This could change your life. It changed mine. Talk to a financial advisor.

Invest in yourself. You may have heard of the 3 percent rule: invest 3 percent of your income into yourself. Honestly, I think that is very low. It's why my book does not have any boundaries. You know what is best for you, and what you can afford. But keep this in mind. It is funny how we don't think twice about spending fifteen dollars on a meal, twenty dollars on a bar tab, or thirty dollars for a shirt. Why do we always question spending twenty dollars on a book that can improve our lives or fifty dollars for a yoga app for the whole year? Six-dollar beer, no problem. One-dollar bottle of water? Outrageous! One-hundred-dollar bar tab for a night of "fun" and a hangover, no problem. Twenty dollars for a yoga class, WTF?

Learn about money. Stocks, 401(k), cryptocurrency, real estate, compound interest, the list is endless.

I believe everyone should start investing now. Even if you can only put five dollars a month into the stock market, you want to start learning now. Books are great to gain knowledge, but certain things in life you learn a lot better from hands-on experience. By starting out small, you can watch your money go up and down and learn from your mistakes without losing too much. Simple advice for new investors:

- Only invest what you can afford to lose.
- Do not sell when stocks are plummeting. Buy.
- Only buy stocks you believe will be around when you die.
- Diversify. Don't put all your money into one stock.
- This is not the lotto, do not invest to get rich quick. Don't get caught up in finding the next Amazon or Bitcoin. Invest for retirement.
- Don't avoid stocks or crypto with high prices. Because some-

thing is $2,000 a share doesn't mean you can't invest five dollars in it. Also, just because a stock is one cent a share doesn't mean it is a good investment. Do your research!
- Read articles with opposing views before you form an opinion. For every article I read about Bitcoin going to the moon, I try to read an article about Bitcoin going to zero.

Remove the common belief that being rich is bad. Media portrays the rich as evil, greedy, and unhappy. Most rich people are very generous and great all-around people. Money is not bad. If you believe money is bad, wouldn't it still be worth making a bunch of money so you could give it away to help someone else? Money is *not* the root of all evil. Money *is* the root of all charities. Are all charities bad? I think we have taken a Bible verse which has truth and turned it into a misconception. It is *the love* of money that is the root of all kinds of evil (Timothy 6:10).

Remove the belief that you need money to be happy. The happiest times of my life were when I was making below minimum wage. You have to find what you love to do. If you have a job you love and are living a life that satisfies you, you don't need massive amounts of money to make you happy. At the same time, do not justify your laziness because you think it is noble to be poor. Be happy with what you have, and if you want more out of life, don't wish or hope for it. Work harder and go get it!

Do not ever say, "If I only won the lotto." Or, "If I only invested in X when it was $ a share." Especially if you do not even play the lotto or invest! I hear this at least once a week. Form a plan to make money. There is enough money to go around.

GBL TIP

My first home cost $8,000 (a sailboat). Under $700 a month for a year, then my house was paid off! You do not always have to do what everyone else is doing. What are other ways you could save a boatload of money? (Pun intended.)

GBL CHALLENGE

How much money will you save after you quit your bad habits, addictions, and time-wasting activities? Start putting that money into a stock, crypto, or ETF that you research. It's a win-win situation. All the money you would have wasted will now be invested. So even if all your investments (because you will diversify, right?) go to zero, you still will at least have quit your bad habit. You can't lose this game! But before you play this game, use the money you save to get out of debt.

PHYSICAL

I have always asked my coworkers who were in shape and older than me what they did to stay fit. It is always the same answer: stay active and watch what you eat. There is never any miracle diet or extreme workout plan involved. Start asking people you would want to look like what kind of workout routine and diet they follow.

Mindful Eating + Daily Movement = Happy Body

GET BUSY LIVING DIET

Stop thinking of the word *diet* as something you have to go on to lose weight. Start thinking of your diet as habitual nourishment. It is what you eat, not what you cannot eat.

Ever go to a bookstore and see entire rows of bookshelves dedicated to different diets? If one diet was the answer, wouldn't there only be a couple of books? There is no magic diet. You must create your own diet that works for your specific body. A diet that allows you to remain at a comfortable weight for the rest of your life without feeling like you are making a huge sacrifice.

GBL Diet. Try to eat only things that come from the ground, a tree, or an animal. Nothing fried, or that comes in a box. Stay away from anything that has to be cooked in a microwave. Sugars are your enemy, even if they come from something you think is healthy like juice. Carbohydrates should be avoided but not shunned. Saturated and trans fats bad, mono- and polyunsaturated fats good. Easy as that.

Know what you are eating. Just because something is marketed as healthy doesn't mean it *is* healthy. A lot of things you may think are healthy actually are not. Fat-free does not mean healthy! Buying your brownies from a healthy foods store doesn't make them healthy. Chocolate chip cookie dough flavored "smart" gelato is probably not really that good for you, even if you think it sounds fancy. Eat a freaking apple if you need a snack.

Educate yourself on what all those numbers and big words on the back of food packaging really mean. You will be surprised, once you are able to interpret the labels, that most foods you thought were good for you are surprisingly horrible.

Make a plan tonight about what you will eat tomorrow. Eventually you will find what foods work with your body, and you won't need to plan.

Here is what I eat every day: eggs, spinach, salmon, tuna, chicken, almonds, cheese (not processed!), broccoli, and blueberries. I try to stay away from foods you have to microwave, but sometimes you need quick and easy meals. My go-to meal is microwaved grilled chicken and a bag of mixed veggies. Nuke the veggies for four minutes in the bag, and the chicken for three minutes, and you have a full meal.

My other emergency food that is great for living full-time on the road is CLIF BARs. They are not healthy (twenty-one grams of sugar = bad), but many times they have saved me from eating fast food (which is worse).

Obviously my diet contains a lot more (living on an airplane for half my life limits me on always eating super healthy), but these are my go-to foods. The good thing about when you get to the point of maintaining your weight is you don't have to count calories or be a complete food snob. I basically eat whatever I want, while trying my best to stick to the GBL Diet. But this only works because I exercise five times a week as well. (Don't get discouraged, my exercise plan is easy as well.)

GBL TIPS

Start small. Cut out something. No fast food on weekdays. No cream and sugar in coffee. No regular Coke. Then start cutting back even more. You should not eat for the sake of pleasure every single meal. You eat to get full. Once a week, eat whatever you want.

If you don't like to cook, find meals that don't require that many ingredients or effort. Beware of the smoothie with fifteen ingredients, that costs forty-five dollars, takes twenty-five minutes to make, and looks like a ninja turtle crapped in a cup. Especially if you don't like cooking! Look for easy meals (not processed food) that you can have ready if you get hungry. When you're hungry, you are not going to want to cook a healthy meal. Don't allow yourself to get hungry.

Do not turn a healthy meal into a fattening one. Do not put fattening dressing on salad. Do not dip vegetables into ranch dressing. Most dressings are not good for you, try lime juice or just eat your greens like Popeye would, plain. Quit acting like a child complaining that the broccoli doesn't taste good. Do not pour cheese all over your broccoli. Stop putting salt, butter, and sugar on everything. Try dipping veggies in a healthy mustard if you must dip them in something. Sounds gross, but it's delicious.

Keep almonds around, plain almonds, no salt or added sugar! When I am starving is the only time I eat fattening meals that I don't plan. By keeping almonds around, you can always bring your stomach back to a rational-thinking-organ state beaver.

Keep track of what you eat. Write down everything you eat for a minimum of two weeks. Research everything you are eating. Add up the calories, fat, sugar, carbs, etc. Post everything you eat on social media (if you love social media). Even if you are in great health, I encourage you to do this if you never have before.

Walk to the store. If you have to carry your groceries home, you will only buy the essentials. I don't care where you live and what season it is—walk. And always go to the store on a full stomach.

Do not finish what's on your plate. This is an outdated tradition from the past. If you can afford to read this book, slow down the pace at which you eat, and stop eating when you are full. If you feel you need to finish your plate because there are starving kids in some other country, then start a charity that ships all your leftover food to that country. Or send it to the kids in your own country.

Drink more water. If you think water does not taste good, then you have never been thirsty. Stop acting like a child and learn to enjoy plain water. I challenge anyone who is a drinker of alcohol or large amounts of Coke (any kind of pop/soda) to try to drink a six-pack of water bottles. Why is it so easy to drink a six-pack of beer, but so hard to drink a six-pack of water?

> **GBL CHALLENGE**
>
> **Do not step on a scale for a year.** Your body changes weight throughout the day. It's a stupid way for people to try to get excited about how much weight they are losing on a quick-loss misery diet. Want to know if you lost weight? Look in the mirror. Are your clothes too big for you now? Remember the biggest benefit to keeping a healthy diet and losing weight is about how you will feel. Not how you look, or a stupid number on a machine.

GET BUSY LIVING WORKOUT ROUTINE

If you want a healthy and happy body, the second part of the equation after mindful eating is moving your body. Why work out? Because muscle burns fat. You don't need to be jacked to burn muscle, every bit of fat you can turn into muscle is moving in the right direction.

Exercise works best if you have a plan on how to implement it: Create your plan to start moving every day. Sweat every day. Work out every day. Take the stairs instead of the elevator. Do something.

You don't have to walk or run for hours to get back into shape. That is the slowest way to get into shape. If you love walking or running, great, keep doing it. But most people dread long cardio, so if you're most people, find a HIIT (high-intensity interval training) exercise or workout to do.

An essential step to making exercise a part of your life is creating a minimum goals for the day (MGFD). I recommend push-ups. Set a number of push-ups you could do no matter what happens in your life. I do ten push-ups every morning. I can always at least achieve my MGFD. If you can't do one push-up, then do it on your knees. If that is still too difficult, do standing push-ups against the wall.

The purpose of the MGFD is not to do ten push-ups a day. The reason we do this is to get the mind into the habit of moving. If you do your ten push-ups, or whatever is easy enough for you, you have a better chance of remembering to go to the gym or do your other workout.

Now, create a sustainable plan you would like to follow for the rest of your life. My goal is simply to go to the gym or start my hotel room workout five times a week. If I go to the gym and realize I don't feel like working out, I still maintained my goal, and I still kept the habit alive of going to the gym. Some of my best workouts have been on days when I had zero motivation to go to the gym. Other times, I have been really motivated to go to the gym, did one set and realized I was tired and not in the mood, and left after that one set. But I still considered it a win. I'm not trying to be the world's strongest man, I only want to feel happy in my body, and stay that way for life.

Get Busy Living Hotel Room Workout. This workout can be done anywhere, anytime. You can do it while you're cooking, watching your favorite sports team, during study breaks, in your room in the morning, literally anywhere. I try to do this small workout even on my off/rest days, just to do something. I don't consider it a failure if I don't do it, though.

One to five rounds. Push-ups, squats, plank, mountain climbers.

Easy as that. You decide the reps. You decide how many rounds.

Try to plan your reps so you fail on the last round. If you only have time for one round, do each exercise until complete failure.

This workout will not get you on a magazine cover, but it will keep your metabolism firing. This is key to losing weight or keeping it off. Your results reflect how hard you work. Remember, doing *something* is always a thousand times better than doing nothing.

GBL TIPS

Keep your workouts interesting. There are hundreds of different types of push-ups, squats, planks, and other HIIT exercises you could do. Mix up the routine from time to time. Also, when you are in the gym, search for new exercises that you enjoy.

Learn about health and fitness. Nothing changes as much as the trends in dieting and exercising. New exercises are fun, and if you find a new food to add to your diet, great. Read books and articles about foods and exercises. Keep in mind anything you see that is marketed as the new superfood or a quick way to lose weight is just a tactic for someone to make money. If you want to add that food or exercise to your diet or workout, great.

Fill in the blank. Yoga is for _____s. If you chose a word that wasn't something positive, I highly recommend giving yoga a try. My body is only slightly more flexible than a steel pipe. I used to think yoga was for ___s. I remember my first week of doing the P90X extreme workout program and being thankful when yoga day came. I thought it would be easy, a day off of stretching. Little did I know it would turn into an hour of torture, cursing, and sweating.

From that day I had a completely new respect for yoga, and I've actually come to enjoy some of the poses. It is still a great workout, and it's becoming less torture. I still feel weird doing some of the poses, but it's also weird at first for a quarterback to stick his hand up a guy's butt to get a ball.

You don't need to go to a class to enjoy yoga. There are many free videos or great apps out there, and you can do it all in the comfort and privacy of your home or hotel room. Once you get comfortable with the poses and some of the names, now you are ready to try a class. I recently got the courage to try a class, and it has changed my life.

Lifting weights is for _____s. Does the thought of lifting weights bring to mind images of really dumb people grunting, sweating, flexing, and taking mirror selfies? These are false stereotypes. There is nothing stupid about taking care of your body.

If you don't work out with weights because you are afraid of getting huge muscles, trust me, you have nothing to worry about. There is an art and science to building muscle, and unless you are working out with huge weights and taking in mass amounts of protein, you will not gain muscle like a bodybuilder.

If you don't lift weights because you don't own any, get yourself to a gym. If you don't want to go to a gym because you're afraid of what people will think of your body, put your ego aside—no one cares what you look like. People only care about themselves. I don't only mean people in the gym, but in all areas of life. Stop worrying what people think about you. The fit people are never going to judge your body, or make you feel like you don't belong. Find a gym that fits you. Not all gyms are full of bodybuilders.

Remember: most people do not like going to the gym. I would say only one in every one hundred times I have gone to the gym, I really wanted to go. You just have to go.

"Lobby in ten?" Most of us pilots like to meet up after a long flight for a beer (hence the catchphrase, "Lobby in ten?"). Now, before I lose all my pilot friends, I want to be clear that I don't think there is anything wrong with having a beer with the crew after a long day. Just start going to the gym first!

In my job, every day is a long day. Don't get in the habit of going out to eat and drink every single time you land. If the first thing I do when I get into my hotel room is start watching videos or make plans to "meet in ten" for beers, I will not go to the gym. If I have a plan in my mind to immediately change into my workout clothes, and when I get to my room, I change clothes, I always go to the gym.

The same is true for any job. Having dinner and a drink with your colleagues is a great way to build camaraderie. Just don't start a bad habit and use the excuse of building camaraderie as the reason you are drinking every night instead of taking care of your body.

Sleep. As an international long-haul cargo pilot, I have no business talking about sleep. Circadian rhythms? I wish. We have to watch a video about fatigue every year, and it gives us this nice briefing about how important getting eight hours of sleep at the same time every night is (basically your circadian rhythm). Then we start making jokes about how impossible this is in our job. No excuses here, we can't do it during our work rotation, which is anywhere from fourteen to thirty-two days. But at least on my month off, I try to get on a good schedule. Like every other section in this book, you can read an entire book about how important sleep is. Here is a quick introduction. Try to get eight hours of uninterrupted sleep in a dark and quiet room. Stay away from caffeine, alcohol, exercise, TV, etc., before bed. Sounds impossible right? I agree, this is an area I am still trying to figure out. Hopefully your life has a little more routine to it, and you can form a good plan for a proper night's sleep.

GBL CHALLENGE

Keep track of your exercise and eating habits. For each day, give yourself either -0.1 for a good day or +0.1 for a bad day. Cheat day can count as 0. Then at the end of the year, add up your score. I bet it's pretty close to the weight you lost (or gained), if you are being honest. It will obviously be different if you are trying to put on muscle (or in my case, I'm trying to maintain my current fitness level).

CLEAN UP YOUR MESS!

MENTAL, EMOTIONAL, SOCIAL, SPIRITUAL

These four categories can be grouped into one big Mess. Most of our problems in life come from problems in one or all of these categories, whether it is something from the past, or something in the present.

These four categories are important to pay attention to at all times. This is not a one-time fix. Every day you need to check in with yourself, and ask what you can do to fix your Mess. Next time you find yourself saying, "Why is my life such a mess right now?", it is because something is off with your Mess.

Fill in the blank. Keeping a journal is for _____s. Physically writing something daily with pen and paper is possibly one of the best medicines out there. It can relieve anger, anxiety, depression, or stress issues. Seeing your thoughts on paper could change your life.

There are so many benefits to keeping a daily journal. My MGFD is to write one sentence. This is also the most important aspect of this book. You have to write things down for this book to work. Writing your feelings down when you are not having the best day is a great way of venting to yourself. Sometimes seeing your worries or fears on paper can make them seem harmless.

I'm not good at _____. Anytime you hear yourself saying this or thinking this, stop yourself. You are only not good at something because you haven't learned how to do it, or you have not practiced it enough. I also used to say I didn't know anything about money because they never taught us in school. After reading a few books, I turned my financial situation around within months. Never stop learning.

Figure out what is stopping you from achieving your goals. Personally, my biggest challenges for writing this book were procrastination and perfectionism. I would have never finished this book if I continued my old ways of putting things off. Even when I got in a good habit of writing a minimum of one thousand words a day, I still would have never finished. I wanted this book to be perfect, but it only kept getting longer and not any better. I cut 120,000 words from my original draft (you're welcome).

Keep a positive attitude. Even if you are having a bad day, try to find something to be thankful for. Try making goofy faces at yourself in the mirror. Watch a comedian you like. Hey Rambo, try screaming into a pillow or crying. Let it all out, man. Remember, some days are just going to be completely janked. No one can avoid days like these. Just accept the jankyness and wait for it to pass.

Adopt a beginner's mindset. It is easy to become conditioned over the years to situations that have become normal. Remember how excited you were the first day of your job? Or your first date? I know this seems hard or stupid. But just try it. Tomorrow try to go about your day like it's the first time you have ever experienced each moment. You don't have to pretend like you have never met Sally or Sue, just, in your own thoughts, try to remember how you felt on your first day.

I was a miserable traveler for a while because I had the attitude that I had already seen everything. I completely missed out on enjoying traveling to some amazing places! You have to live each moment like it is: a new moment. Stop comparing the present moment, or you will never be happy.

Focus. Focusing on the task in front of you is vital to success. When doing tasks that require a lot of concentration (studying, reading, writing, etc.), give yourself a mental break. I use the Pomodoro technique. Set a twenty-five-minute timer and then take a five-minute break. It's the little things in life that can make the biggest differences. This was a huge key in procrastination for me. It allowed me to stop, realize if I was still focused on the task, or if I had zoned out. Get a cheap watch with a timer on it so you don't have to reach for your phone, which is likely to distract you. Set a timer for five minutes and take a thirty-second break if you need to really stay focused.

You need to be more selfish. Helping others and being around family and friends is great. But you have to take care of yourself first. If everyone took care of their own needs, it would make the world a better place. Learn to say no.

Loneliness is a temporary feeling. Social media will not cure loneliness, dating will not cure it, eating will not cure it, romantic comedies will not cure it, alcohol with not cure it, sex will not cure it. The best way to deal with temporary feelings of loneliness is to follow your dreams. If you are lonely, it only means your life is temporarily without passion. By passion I don't mean romantic passion. This is the same with boredom. It's only a temporary feeling. Once you set up your life plan in the next chapter, there will be little room for boredom or loneliness. These are normal human feelings—don't be afraid of them. Don't be afraid of being alone.

Fear is behind everything that is holding you back in life. Learn to admit you are afraid. Learn to face your fears. I'm not talking about admitting you are afraid of snakes. I'm talking about the fear of not being yourself. Being afraid of others judging you. Fear of being alone. Fear of failure. Fear of rejection. Fear of letting others down. What fears are holding you back from chasing your true passions? **WRITE DOWN YOUR FEARS.**

You are unlucky. Have you grown up thinking there is a curse against your family's name? This type of thinking is the easiest way to stay stuck where you are. Stop this thinking and realize that life throws unlucky circumstances at everyone. Some things we may never understand (for example, death), but you have to make peace with those things and realize they are a part of everyone's life. Stop feeling sorry for yourself.

Do not compare yourself to others. Never look at someone else's life and wish you could be like them. You have no idea what is really going on in their life. People put on a happy face around others and especially on social media. This is not necessarily a bad thing. If you are having a bad day, Mr. Grumpy, don't ruin my good day!

Learn to laugh at yourself. If laughter is the best medicine, then why not give yourself a dose of it every time you trip on an invisible obstacle? Try not to self-deprecate yourself by thinking you are stupid or not worthy. Just laugh about it and enjoy the fact that you are a human.

The power of giving compliments. Next time you are at a restaurant or at the checkout counter, tell someone that you love their name (even if you hate it), and watch their reaction. You will both have a better day because of it. Do not tell Joe he has a unique and pretty name, instead find something else about him to compliment. Tell a coworker their hair looks amazing today, or they look great in those new glasses.

Take a "free!" personality test. Find out what areas in life you are strong in and what needs improvement. Try to become a more balanced person. For me, I am learning how to talk. Literally. As an introvert, I am just not good at speaking, and I am finding out that this is one of the biggest things holding me back. I can improve my communication skills; I just need to learn about the subject.

Fill in the blank. Getting in touch with your feelings or soul searching is for _____s. This may sound so weird to us "tough" guys and gals. But we all need to do it. We need to figure out all the crap that is going on inside our head. Come up with a new name if you must, but we all need to figure out our emotions. Tame The Beast?

Go to a men's or women's group, try therapy, or do what I did and lock yourself in a room in Thailand for three weeks and write a book about why you can't quit your addictions! This is not an easy thing to do. Facing all of the feelings we have locked up in a dark place inside ourselves for so many years is scary. But this is key to freeing ourselves. Being able to open up and talk to someone about this is great; if you are not ready to do that, then at least be honest and open with yourself.

Forgiving is easy, learn to forget. You can't forgive someone if you constantly bring it up every time you get in a fight with that person. Don't hold grudges.

Improve your communication and listening skills. This is a deeper subject than it appears. Everyone knows you should try not to interrupt someone. Everyone thinks they are a good listener. But if you improve the way you communicate, it could clean up your Mess in ways you can't believe. It seems like a boring subject, but search for books on communication, and you might be surprised how much room for improvement there is.

Become interesting. I don't mean act a fool or be the loudest person in the room. Learn how to ask better questions and give more interesting answers. If someone asks what you do for a living, don't just say, "Sales." I like to tell people I fly neon-green hair dye from Anchorage, Alaska to Guangzhou, China. Or I fly pigs from Nairobi to Istanbul. Because it's true.

Your job. I don't care if you think you are better than the job you are working right now. Be the best damn bag boy in the land (TBDBITL, go Bucks!). Once you master the art of separating the canned corn from the smashables, ask for a promotion. Do not get stuck being comfortable being the best damn bag boy. Continue to challenge yourself and enjoy the feeling of being a beginner again. Look forward to the fulfillment of going from the struggles of learning something new to mastering it.

Remember that the people you hang out with the most will influence you the most. The more you keep moving up, the better influences you will have. Don't be afraid to take the next step. Form good working habits now, and you will be rewarded in the future.

Build, improve, and repair your relationships. No one has a perfect relationship with their family, friends, or coworkers. Maybe the problem is not only the other person's fault. Take a hard look at yourself first and be curious to see if you could change your ways at all. Next, take a look at their personality. Take a personality test and try to answer the questions as if you were that person, and maybe you'll find that there is a different way you could relate to them.

If that person is completely against change or compromise, maybe it is time to remove them from your life. I know a guy in Miami who will do this for a small fee…Just kidding.

Don't assume you are the world's greatest dad, wife, or boss because everyone seems to like you, and you have a coffee mug that says so. Read books on whatever you are or want to be. Learn how to be a better boss, employee, parent, or partner.

Tap into your spiritual side. And you thought there were a lot of diets out there! Find what works for you and don't judge others. I don't care whether you are religious or not—meditation, prayer, or quiet time is good for all of us. Whether you believe in God, the universe, or the Invisible Pink Unicorn, learn to accept other people's beliefs and don't try to force your beliefs onto someone.

Fill in the blank. Meditation is for _____s. If you used a word to describe something you would not want to be, then I highly advise you to give this a chance. You can't read one self-help book these days without some sort of mention of meditation or mindfulness. And there is a reason. It works.

But if you are like me, and you can't sit in the lotus position for more than forty-five seconds, then I have good news. You don't have to sit perfectly still in the lotus position for an hour while humming or chanting. You can get the benefits from starting small. Mindfulness is key to this book. All this means is that you have to start becoming aware of your feelings and your evil little ego.

I know, Rambo was probably never aware of his feelings, but he wasn't a very happy guy either. The only way to stop bad habits and start new positive habits is to stop yourself before you make the unconscious decision to do something that doesn't benefit your goal. Take a quick meditation each day, and instead of or after a body scan, ask yourself how you are doing in each area. How could you get better? Try to spend a couple of seconds on each category of F.P. Messy.

GBL CHALLENGE

The next time you feel lonely or bored, try to sit and clear your mind. Realize you are bored or lonely and have nothing to do. Rejoice that you have nothing to do. Sit and meditate on how wonderful it is that you have nothing at all to do at this moment. If you find yourself unable to sit still, stand, or lie down, then go for a walk. Sometimes you just need to sit and quiet your mind, sometimes your body just needs to move. Maybe you need a laugh and to move. Watch a Richard Simmons video.

YOU (OR YOUR PASSIONS)

This category is for anything that you want to improve or to do more of. It would be impossible to list every possibility in this book, but you know what you want to become better at (or else you wouldn't be reading this book). Do you want to be more organized, keep a clean living or workspace, improve personal hygiene, stop procrastinating? All those things can go here.

If you want to clean or organize your house, don't try to organize an entire drawer a day. Organize one thing from one drawer for your MGFD. You may find yourself cleaning the entire kitchen in one go. Or just throw away the seventeen-year-old book of matches from Chi-Chi's. The point is to do something so small you have no excuse not to do it. Clean just one thing. Start cleaning the back of one ear. The purpose of this is sometimes you will be in the mood to do more. Sometimes you won't. Keep the habit alive even on days when you are not fully motivated, or you simply do not have the time in your schedule that day.

In Part IV, we will talk about finding and following your passions. Add your passions to this list, or anything you have always wanted to do. It could be anything. Spend more time with the grandkids or learn to scuba dive. Start a business or learn to play the didgeridoo.

This is not a bucket list. Don't choose things that other people have done that you want to do so you can buy the T-shirt. Ask yourself why you want to visit one hundred countries or go skydiving. Is it for bragging rights? Or do you actually have one hundred countries you really want to see? Do you really want to jump out of a perfectly good airplane? Or do you just think it would be cool to post on social media?

The point here—in fact, the point of this whole book—is to build a life that allows you to live to your full potential. A life that allows you to be your true self, full of courage and confidence. We're not aiming to create a perfect life that will look great on social media, or that you can brag about to the people you are trying to impress, but a life that makes *you* feel truly fulfilled.

If you're like most people, then you haven't spent much time asking yourself what you really want or what truly makes you happy. This section is your opportunity to start. Remember after making your list to ask yourself *why* you really want all those things. Do you want a big house because you have twenty kids? Or you love to clean so much you want more rooms to clean? Maybe you want a big house to throw massive parties for your friends? I would say those are all legit ideas.

Try to differentiate between a goal/dream and a fantasy. Most of my bicycle rides in Florida take me past mansions on the beach or beautiful, huge houses in Coconut Grove. Of course

I fantasize about living in a house like that. But when I really think about how much it would cost just to do the landscaping, I have second thoughts. Would I really just want to sit at my house and admire it? No, therefore my dream is to make enough money to rent a mansion on the beach for a couple weeks or a month. People might think I'm wasting money by spending tens of thousands of dollars for a few weeks, but really I'm saving millions!

But, of course, ideas and dreams are meaningless without execution. MGFD are a good start to implementing change in your life, but to truly revolutionize how you live, you need a game plan. That's what we will create in the next part.

Rowing to my first home! 31' Bombay Clipper. Dinner Key Marina, Miami, Florida.

One of my first camping trips. Eleuthera, Bahamas.

Walking to my FREE! paradise. I had to pay extra for the sand fleas. Exuma, Bahamas.

A lonesome trip to Neil Island, India. $1 hostel felt like a prison camp.

Smoking bidi's and drinking alcohol known to make people go blind. My friends decided we should leave after some drunk threw a bottle at my head. Jaipur, India.

Some of the best times of my life. Bartending in Cambodia with some of my favorite people in one of my favorite locations. Sorry, if you Google Koh Ru/Bamboo Island it no longer is a hostel. It is now a $300 a night resort!

Back in my Rambo days! Shooting AK-47 at 8:00 in the morning. I woke up in a tuk-tuk thinking I would be eating breakfast, instead I got a menu full of guns, rocket launchers, and you could even buy a cow (to shoot with the rocket launcher). Near Phnom Penh, Cambodia.

YOU (OR YOUR PASSIONS) · 101

Making one of my Swiss Family Robinson dreams come true. Riding an Ostrich near Nairobi, Kenya.

Facing one of my fears. Teaching English in Sri Lanka.

This is where I wrote the first draft of this book in three weeks. I went back a few months later and learned to sail! Ao Yon Beach, Thailand.

PART III

GAME PLAN FOR WINNING LIFE

There are many ways to plan your life. You can make a to-do list, you can try to schedule your entire day, week, or month. You can create a vision board. You can follow one of the other ten thousand life plans out there.

The key is to find what works best for you.

I created the Get Busy Living Plan because none of the other traditional ways worked for me. The GBL Plan allows plenty of room for changes. I work a month on/month off flying schedule. During my month on, it is laughable to try to plan anything. I never know what time zone or country I will be in next, and it is impossible to have a normal sleep schedule. This is where the GBL Plan has turned my life around. We can't prepare for all the surprises life will throw at us, and it is easy to become overwhelmed with our life circumstances. Having a written-out plan keeps me focused on my priorities and goals in life. No matter how busy or crazy my schedule gets, I can at least accomplish my MGFD and keep the habits alive until my life returns to "normal."

The setup for your personal GBL Plan is up to you. This is the format I use, feel free to copy it. The point is, everyone is different, and this format is flexible enough for you to add anything else to your plan that you find necessary or motivating.

Here are the steps I follow:

- Step 1: Revisit your list of F.P. Messy ideas.
- Step 2: Ask yourself questions.
- Step 3: Set periodic goals (MGFD, but also daily, monthly, yearly, lifetime, and achievements).

- Step 4: Create a mission statement and find mantras and values that reflect your life.

I will explain these steps in depth, so you understand the thinking behind each and how they come together in a GBL Plan. Then I'll show you what a sample GBL Plan can look like, so that you have it clear in your head.

STEP 1: REVISIT YOUR LIST OF F. P. MESSY IDEAS

Hopefully in the previous chapter you already completed this step and figured out anything you wanted to improve on. Add as many ideas as you like here; at this point, the more the better. In the next step, you will prioritize. But for now, just **WRITE DOWN** anything you can think of you would like to do, or things you could improve in the near or distant future.

Example F.P. Messy ideas:

F Start a budget. Form a plan to get out of debt. Read a beginners book about money. Do an online retirement calculator.

P Cut out cream and sugar in coffee and eating after 8:00 p.m. Get a gym membership, go to the gym four times a week and do one exercise machine. Do one sun salutation (yoga) every morning. Try something new like CrossFit, kickboxing, paddleboarding, tai chi, rollerblading, surfing, etc.

Mess Journal one sentence every day. Smile at or compliment one person each day. Meditate or pray one minute daily. Read a book about improving relationships with coworkers. Learn something new: candle making, painting, a musical instrument, a new language, etc.

Y Write three books. Learn to scuba dive. Spend more time with family. Learn to sail. Read a book on how to stop procrastinating (or take Nike's advice and Just Do It!). Start a business. Keep my living and workspace organized. Airbnb a castle on the beach with a waterslide and monkeys who serve me mint tea in full uniform.

STEP 2: ASK YOURSELF QUESTIONS

By "ask yourself questions," I mean five questions in particular that are going to help you frame your GBL Plan. Remember, this is *your* plan. Feel free to ask any additional questions you think would benefit your life, or give you a better indication of the kind of life you want to live.

Under your list of F.P. Messy ideas write down (or type) the following questions:

- What are my priorities?
- What excuses am I making?
- What are my fears?
- What can I do about it?
- Did I get better today? Or, did I win today?

For the first question, take a look back at your F.P. Messy list and prioritize what is most important to you. You don't have to prioritize everything, but identify the critical points you want to focus on. Then make a list of what you would like to accomplish above anything else. These could be anything ranging from small things like responding to an email, to big work projects or relationship issues.

Next, think about what excuses you are making and what fears are holding you back. Be brutally honest with yourself. Write them down so that you're clear about the obstacles in your path. Fears and excuses are your biggest enemy when attempting to do anything meaningful in your life. If you don't know who the enemy is, you can't win the battle. This is one of the most difficult things we face in life, but we must take control of our fears and excuses. By making them known and becoming aware of fears and excuses, they become less intimidating and, eventually, it might even seem silly that you ever had those thoughts in the first place.

Next, ask yourself, "What can I do about it?" Take a clear look at your fears and excuses and write down how you can face them. Often these won't be actionable items, but just things you need to keep in mind, or you find a new way of looking at the problem.

For example, I had a fear of going to a yoga class because I wasn't flexible. I thought I would get laughed at and kicked out of the class because I couldn't twist myself into a Half Lord of the Fishes pose. I feared I would get made fun of when I cried tears of torture during the Happy Baby pose. But once I wrote this down, I realized I was being dramatic. And guess what? Going to a yoga class was nothing like the other sports I played. No one yelled at me, even during my Downward Dog that looks like Deformed Cow. Everyone was encouraging, and the other day my instructor told me I had a beautiful practice (whatever that means). It didn't make me feel the most manly I've ever felt, but damn if I didn't feel like a happy little pretzel walking out of class that day.

Another example: if you make an excuse that you are too lazy to do something, then your answer to "What can I do about it?" could be to start remembering that laziness is not a condition or disease. Humans are only lazy because being lazy is comfortable. Laziness will never lead to a truly fulfilling and happy life. Make your GBL Plan and start actively pursuing something.

The answer to "What can I do about it?" could be as simple as remembering that there is really nothing to fear or there is no valid excuse to be made. Reframing, or looking at the problem from a different angle, can be powerful in showing you whether it's a problem at all.

Finally, ask yourself, "Did I get better today?" One key to this book is stacking good days. Ask yourself if you made progress and be honest. Can you consider today a win? Once you start to have more good days than bad days, you gain confidence. When you gain confidence, you start to believe in yourself and transform into the person you were truly meant to be.

In the next step, we learn how to set goals. Except I hate calling them goals because every book I've read about setting goals or forming habits has not worked for me in the long term due to my unpredictable schedule and lifestyle of living on the road. Now, before you call me out for breaking Rule #3 (No excuses!), I didn't accept this excuse and settle for a life of mediocrity and selling myself short. I created the Get Busy Living Plan and in particular minimum goals for the day (MGFD) to keep these goals and habits alive. Read on!

STEP 3: SET PERIODIC GOALS

After you have created your list of things you want to improve (accomplished in Step 1), it is time to divide those items into periodic goals. Here are the different categories of goals:

- Minimum goals for the day
- Daily goals
- Monthly goals
- Yearly goals
- Lifetime goals
- Achievements

The trick here is to prioritize. The goals with the most priority will move up and become your minimum goals for the day, while the others can be pushed to monthly, yearly, or lifetime goals. Here's a more in-depth explanation of each category.

1. MINIMUM GOALS FOR THE DAY

Figure out your main priorities in life. Where do you want to improve the most, or what do you want to turn into a habit?

These are what you will turn into your minimum goals for the day (MGFD).

As you might recall from the last section, your MGFD are what you do every single day, without excuses.

If you want to read more, just open a book and read for one minute. Practice the guitar for one minute. Eat one piece of fruit. Do only ten push-ups (it reminds your body it needs to work out). Sometimes the push-ups are not comfortable, but do them anyway. This teaches you toughness. One of my MGFD is to study ten questions or one page of notes as a minimum. I have recurrent training every year and have random line checks where someone watches everything I do during the whole flight. This can be stressful unless you stay prepared; my MGFD keeps the knowledge I need fresh in my mind.

Make up your own MGFD, set a time to do them, and enjoy the reward of the satisfaction of getting something done. You don't need candy or cigarettes anymore. This is the first step in changing your whole life around. It's going to be amazing. Be creative, make your own rules.

The only rule I have is to make sure it is something so simple you can do every day without any excuse. Also try to do the things that take the least amount of time first. Making your bed will always take ten seconds. Ten push-ups will only take twenty seconds.

All my MGFD together can be completed in under ten minutes. This gives me absolutely no excuses for not at least accomplishing these goals. It may not be as much as I would like to do, but I at least kept the action alive to someday turn it into a habit. I try to do my MGFD first thing in the morning, as knowing I already accomplished something gives me motivation for the day.

2. DAILY GOALS

Your daily goals should reflect your MGFD. Just because it is a daily goal doesn't mean you have to do it every day. Come up with your own unique plan. For example, you can have a daily goal of working out, but if you only want to work out four days a week, there will be days you don't need to hit this goal.

Think it is impossible to find X amount of time in your day to accomplish all these activities? Did you read Part I of this book?! How much time are you wasting? If you have no extra time, and you work twenty hours a day, you should seriously consider quitting your job and finding a new employer or profession. How are you reading this if you have no time?

3. MONTHLY GOALS

Monthly goals are things you only want to do once or twice a month. I started sketching one thing a month. I hope someday I will start to do it more, but my minimum is once a month.

If you are good at setting an exact date (say every first of the month), then do your monthly goals on that date. If you have a random schedule, then try to time the goals with an event. I travel every month, and so I always sketch something from my travels in my journal. Or do your budget on payday. Find something that will trigger you to do your goal (not many of us forget payday!).

4. YEARLY GOALS

Yearly goals are things you want to achieve in the near future. These goals have the biggest chance of failure. So, instead of just writing them down, book them.

Don't just dream of a trip to Shangri La. Book it. Buy the airline tickets, book the hotel.

Don't just say you will take an ice bath. Set a date and make yourself accountable. December 25, 2022, I will take an ice bath and post pictures on social media. I don't have social media, so I met a couple who became my accountability partners, and I will send them a Merry Christmas message of me in an ice bath. (Don't worry guys, I will wear shorts.)

Set ridiculous goals. I set a goal to finish the book I had been writing for the last fifteen years in three weeks. I did it. Who knew publishing it would take six months! Don't worry so much about the timeframe as the goal itself. If you have to save three years for your trip to El Dorado, it still counts as one of your yearly goals: saving money for it is your goal.

5. LIFETIME GOALS

This is where most people either have no idea what would really make them happy, or they set goals that are someone else's dreams. A good practice is for each goal, ask yourself why you want to achieve that goal. This will help you realize if you truly want something, that your life wouldn't be complete without it, or if it is just something society deems a sign of success. I know I want a dog someday because I love dogs and they bring joy to my life. I want to sail around the world because I love adventure, travel, and the sea. I am still constipated with two more books inside me that will eventually have to come out.

6. ACHIEVEMENTS

Once an MGFD or daily goal becomes something you do every day without even thinking about it, move it into your achievements section. There are two reasons it is beneficial to keep track of your achievements. One, it is good for your confidence to see all the ways you have improved your life. Two, it is good to keep track of achievements in case, for some reason, they stop becoming a habit. For example, while writing this book, I was in a part of Thailand where there is no such thing as a cold shower. So I moved taking a cold shower once a day from my achievements back into my MGFD. Some of my old MGFD routines included:

- Make my bed
- Clear fifty emails a day (when my four email accounts had hundreds to thousands of emails)
- Organize twenty pictures
- Take a shower (just kidding, but if you don't shower daily, you might want to include this)

Also in this section you can include big accomplishments you have achieved, such as learning to scuba dive. Or, something you had to face your fears to accomplish, like smiling at a stranger or going to your first yoga class.

Example GBL Periodic Goals: minimum goals for the day (MGFD), daily, monthly, yearly, and lifetime goals.

MGFD	DAILY	MONTHLY	YEARLY	LIFETIME
Ten push-ups.	Workout (four days/week).	Budget.	Take one ice bath.	Write three books.
Meditate one minute.	Meditate twenty minutes.	Sketch something.	Publish first book.	Get a dog.
Stretch one minute.	Yoga thirty minutes.	Update GBL Plan.	Yoga class/ retreat.	Sailboat.
Study ten questions.	Study Pomodoro.			
Journal one sentence.	Thirty minutes to learn.			

Achievements—Make bed, cold shower, clear fifty emails a day, organize twenty pictures

Most other books on goals will tell you not to set too many goals. I disagree. I think we could use a complete life makeover. Write all your goals down so you can visually refer to them every day. Print out your GBL Plan. Or just write it out. **Keep a copy in your pocket at all times.** You don't have to hit all your goals each day to win. You decide if it was a win or not. Be honest with yourself and every day ask yourself:

Did I win today?

Did I get better today?

It is important to ask yourself these questions each day. Don't be too hard on yourself. If you normally eat fast food three times a day, and today you only ate McDonalds twice, that's a win. You are getting better. You do not have to be perfect all at once. Did you do more positive things than negative? Did you get done what needed to be done? Did you complete your MGFD? Each day that you can answer honestly, "Yes, I got better today, I won today," is a step in the right direction.

STEP 4: CREATE A MISSION STATEMENT AND MANTRAS

Mission statements revolve around your values. Who do you want to be? Part of my mission statement is just listing my values. It doesn't have to be poetically worded. Reading this everyday will keep you focused on what *you* want out of life, and not what others expect you to be or expect you to do.

I believe creating a mission statement, like your Get Busy Living Plan, will be an ongoing process. If you look up examples online, most are geared toward business executives. So keep in mind you can make up whatever you want.

In your mission statement, write down what type of person you want to be at work, with your family, and overall. Write down where you want to be in the future. What goals do you want to achieve? Look up how to write a mission statement. Write why you are quitting your bad habits (unless you think the reminder would decrease your chances of succeeding; for me it helps to remember). Read your mission statement every day.

Find mantras, mottos, slogans, quotes, maxims, phrases, whatever you want to call them, that you can use to keep you focused on your mission statement and game plan. Examples of some of the mantras I use:

- Get busy living!
- No excuses.
- Just Do It. Nike has the simplest, yet most effective slogan to overcome no motivation.
- Through discipline, I get things done.
- If you feed The Beast, it will never die.
- I am ripping my old excuses a new asshole. (See the section at the end of the book under recommendations. This mantra is from *I Am Affirmations: F*ck Procrastination and All Excuses.*)
- Loneliness is temporary.
- Take an LSD trip every day. Learn, see, or do something new.
- Eric against the world (stolen from "Ohio Against The World"). This has to do with football, not myself or Ohio actually taking over the world. It also is a great 2Pac song.

GBL PLAN: EXAMPLE

Once you are finished gathering all the things you want to improve in your life, your Get Busy Living Plan might look something like the example below.

Or it could look totally different! You might recognize a theme throughout the book. And that theme is to never look at things as being the only way to do it. It's nice to have a plan laid out for us (because we are lazy creatures), but remember that no one else's plan will work the same for you. Be creative and find your own way.

I'm not saying other books or methods are bad or wrong. The opposite is true, in fact. I will always continue to read, enjoy, and gain knowledge by reading books or trying new workout plans or different eating habits. My Get Busy Living Plan is constantly changing. One week it looks like the example below, and then I change it to another format that I think works better.

The point is, the GBL Plan is not the only way to get your life in shape. But it has one essential element: it's written down. If you were to take anything new from my book, I would like that to be for you to have a written plan for your life. Something you look at everyday to remind you of your priorities. It should constantly change—there is nothing wrong with realizing something you thought was your dream has now changed.

Not too long ago, I thought my purpose in life was to start a globe museum. I am slightly nerdy when it comes to atlases and globes. I was extremely disappointed when I found out (at least at the last time of searching) that there wasn't a dedicated globe museum in the United States, and only one in the whole world! Thank you, Austria. But for someone who gets antsy being in one location for more than a few days, I realized that having a globe museum would not really be the best thing for me. My dream changed.

You can use the example below as a guideline, but don't be afraid to be creative. Use your imagination! Turn it into a pie chart, put stickers on it, use different colors, tattoo it on your forearm (remember your plan will change though), make the layout vertical instead of horizontal…the possibilities are endless. Do anything with it except try to keep it in your head. **WRITE IT DOWN** and don't forget to combine or keep it with your trigger/contingency plan and pros/cons you made for quitting your addictions.

Remember that while the GBL Plan can be created in a linear fashion (following Step 1 to Step 4), each step also informs the other. In the example below, I rearranged the outline of my GBL Plan to what works best for me. So do not feel confused or frustrated when you read my example below and wonder why it is out of order!

I also expanded on some of the items. For example, I split my MGFD into morning and night, and I added Chinese numbers one to ten (because I want to learn Chinese). I also added my threat/contingency plan and pros/cons from Part 1, although I wrote it in a different format.

Do not get discouraged if my plan seems confusing or long. You are not meant to understand everything written below. A lot of it is shorthand for something that is significant to me. This is just an example of what it could look like. Once you **WRITE DOWN** all your answers to the instructions above, you can invent your own format. You may think mine is too long or unorganized. So simplify it to your liking. Or make it a ten-page flowchart! Don't worry too much about your first draft. Just come back and edit it as often as you like. That's why this plan is flexible and open to change.

AN EXAMPLE OF WHAT A GBL PLAN COULD LOOK LIKE

What are my priorities? Study for training. Study for training. Study for training. Finish book. Study for sailing school. Look into getting a patent for my invention. Find a new accountant to do my taxes. Work out, eat healthy, stretch, run, yoga. Read books on how to communicate better.

MGFD (morning)—ten push-ups, clear emails, one minute stretch, one minute meditation, ten training questions, cold shower, practice tying sailing knots.

1—Yee; 2—Arr; 3—San; 4—Suh; 5—Woo; 6—Leo; 7—Chee; 8—Baa; 9—Geo; 10—Shu-oh

This is how I learned to count to ten in Chinese. Add new words every week/month.

MGFD (night)—journal one sentence, meditate one minute, stretch one minute.

Daily Goals—ten pictures, study POMO, sailing course study, yoga, workout, run, eat healthy.

What excuses am I making? I have an addictive personality. I failed the first time I tried to sail. I can't live without my crutch. My job is too tiring to work out every day. I work hard, so I deserve to be lazy and drink beer every night. I'm not flexible.

What are my fears? My book will suck. I will regret not applying to a different job. I will fail training. I will be lonely and never find another girl who I get along with. I will never learn how to sail. I fear I will not be able to quit smoking. People will make fun of me and judge me in a yoga class.

What can I do about it? Study for training. Remember you know all you need to know. Know you are prepared. Remember you have passed training for the last fifteen years, and you are a good pilot. Remember that nicotine or alcohol doesn't help anything, they only hide a feeling while making you feel shitty later, they don't make the feeling go away. They only make it worse. Realize I am happy at my current company and just because everyone else is applying to different jobs doesn't mean I need to as well. I don't need a girlfriend now; I don't want a girlfriend now. When I am ready and figure out my priorities and passions, then I will meet her. I have never really tried to learn to sail (I can fly a freaking 747 for someone's sake, why not sail a boat?). If I don't write my book, I will always regret it. If my book fails to sell, that was not my goal, my goal was to write a book.

F—Budget, JOMO (joy of missing out), read books, less now/more later.

P—Gym three to four times a week, run every day, under seven-minute mile by age forty, create new workouts.

M—Learn (business, money, sail, knots, Chinese), read books about learning.

E—Journal when and why I have cravings, why do I actually get lonely, what do I really want, who do I want to be?

S—Become interesting, learn to tell more interesting stories, form a tribe, surround myself with positive influences. Read a book on how to communicate better.

S—Meditate. Read books.

Y—Whiten my teeth, enjoy being a nonsmoker, find out if sailing is really a passion, find out if helping people make their lives better is really a passion, Namibia, Israel/Jordan with Dad, visit Kevin in Vietnam, Karin and Frank in Paris, JD and Marlene (wherever they are dog sitting!), Bolivia, Khartoum. Volunteer at a retirement home.

Mission Statement, Values, Mantras
I am constantly getting things done. I do the task at hand and look forward to the satisfaction of getting it done. When stressful thoughts enter my head, I just breathe them away. I get rid of any negative thoughts I have about writing my book or any other fears/doubts. I make excuses for excuses. I am in control of my mind. My ego is evil, but I will not let him win. Nothing he wants to do will actually make me feel better. If you feed The Beast, it will never die. I study a little each day so I am always prepared for training or line checks. I will keep my body in shape and enjoy doing it. I eat healthy because it makes me feel better. Win the first and last hour of every day. I will do anything that needs to be done now instead of later. It is not my job to make other people happy, but I love trying to help. Optimism is contagious. Every day I get better. Every day is a win. Stay humble, stay hungry. Whenever you get comfortable, you are in a dangerous spot. Enjoy the true, good life, the excitement of new challenges to conquer.

As you can see, my mission statement is random gibberish, but it means a lot to me. Make yours however you want. Have fun with it.

VALUES	MANTRAS
Adventure.	Get busy living!
Explore.	No excuses.
Balance.	Just Do It—Nike.
Courage.	Loneliness is temporary.
Growth.	Eric against the world.
Wellness.	
Optimism.	
Fun.	
Be original.	

Monthly Goals—Draw something, write a haiku poem, revise GBL Plan, do something you fear/have been procrastinating, budget.

Yearly Goals—Take an ice bath, learn to sail, finish my book. Namibia, Bolivia, Israel/Jordan with Dad, Visit Kevin in Vietnam, Karin and Frank in Paris, JD and Marlene (wherever they are dog sitting!) Volunteer at a retirement home.

Lifetime Goals—Write three books, dog, sail around the world, family. Khartoum, Congo, Papua New Guinea.

Khartoum, Congo, and PNG will probably not happen next year, but they are on the list for 2024 so I put them under Lifetime Goals.

Achievements—Wrote book, first yoga class, learned to sail, quit smoking! Quit drinking every night, quit biting my nails, made bed, cleared all my email inboxes, taught English in Sri Lanka.

Threats
Wake up, coffee, technology, truck, bored, stress, anxious, tired, unexpected bullshit, change of plans, five o'clock somewhere, being in a new location, after/before work, worst day ever, having to fix something, annoying things that make me want to scream, alcohol, lonely, when with friends, something good or bad happens, seeing someone else do something bad that looks fun, book/movie, going to work, training, being nervous, shitty hotel, shitty weather, being around one person too long, sunsets.

Contingency Plan
MGFD, breathe, Wim Hof, cold shower, brush/whiten teeth, run, read, yoga, workout, GBL Plan, meditate, make a new plan, have a plan, realize you like being in a new location and it's a good feeling, not reason for anxiety or stress, shower, ten push-ups, eat, mints/gum, coffee, tea, journal, budget, don't worry unless it's something that will kill you, bike ride, study, listen to music.

Pros for Quitting
I will not stink, it is messy (ashes, cigarette burns, etc.), I will not feel guilty buying cigarettes or lighting up around other people. I will gain confidence, energy, self-esteem, and my freedom, I will not have to plan my day around the cigarette. I will not feel jittery or have the feeling that something is missing every twenty minutes, it does not cure stress, boredom, anxiety, or depression. I will enjoy my meals more. Smoking leads to drinking, drinking leads to being lazy, it does not help me concentrate. You can't type with a cigarette in your hand. The nicotine gets the credit for making me feel better, but the nicotine is the problem. I will have more time, money, health, and be attractive to my future wife. Would I want her to be a smoker? Hell no! Gross! There are no cons for quitting smoking!

GBL TIPS

Here are a few ways to increase chances of doing your daily routine (and thus sticking to the GBL Plan as a whole):

- Stop looking at your phone first thing in the morning! Try to get your MGFD done before you look at your phone.
- Set a reminder to do your MGFD or other important tasks. The reminder can be on your phone unless you are trying to use your phone less—then use sticky notes.
- Set things out. If you want to make tea in the morning or eat fruit, set it out the night before.
- If quitting something, do the opposite of setting things out: try to make it invisible. If possible, completely remove the distraction.
- Give yourself a cheat day. I bet you find yourself doing your routine even on cheat day! But it gives you a chance to still enjoy your favorite guilty pleasure foods or just have a lazy day. But you will realize it's not that hard to do most of these little things that improve your life. You might be someone who does not do well with the cheat day. If this doesn't work for you, don't do it. Certain things we need to completely cut out.
- Try to always have more wins (more days where you complete most of your tasks) than losses (days where you didn't accomplish your MGFD).
- When reading other self-help books, take notes. Be specific, write the title of the book, page number, and a short message about what you read that you want to remember. **WRITE IT DOWN!**
- Get a cheap watch with a timer function and stopwatch. Use it for timing one minute or Pomodoro (twenty-five minutes). Use the stopwatch to time your bad habits. Stay away from timers on your phone—it's just another chance to get distracted.
- Making a pros and cons list can also be beneficial to many aspects

of life, not just quitting addictions. If you are thinking of switching jobs, moving to a different city, going to school in Arizona or Florida, going to the gym or eating ice cream, watching a movie or reading a book...**WRITE DOWN** the pros and cons.

- Be organized and maintain a clean space. It's amazing how much more I get done when my home or hotel room is organized. When I get to a hotel, I lay out everything for the next day and organize my stuff. You will be less likely to forget things, and you will be able to think more clearly. When the place is clean, it sets the tone to keep your life clean.
- Keep your GBL Plan everywhere. In your pocket, on your refrigerator, inside your suitcase, on your car dashboard, on the back of the toilet lid (don't forget to put the seat down, though), wherever you will see it multiple times a day.

> **GBL CHALLENGES**
>
> 1. Do something big this year. Focus all your effort into getting something done that you have been putting off. Maybe an unfinished college degree or learning a new skill. Start planning a trip you have always wanted to take. Fix the newel post. Only you can decide if you succeed in life. Set huge goals, and if you come up a little short, who cares?
> 2. Do something you are afraid of. I love to do things I am afraid of. Conquering it gives you so much confidence. At least do something out of your comfort zone. It can be simple. Take the bus somewhere. Talk to a stranger. Travel solo. Go rappelling, ride a horse, take a yoga class, volunteer in a different country, skydive, bungee jump, go on a date, move somewhere you always wanted to, try the job you don't think you can do. Come up with your own list. Put at least one of these in your yearly goals and do it!
> 3. Try to keep your email inbox clear. I have four different emails and the majority of the time, I keep them at zero messages. This was a huge help with becoming more efficient. It is similar to keeping a clean work/living environment. Unsubscribe from any useless emails. If I only have five emails in my inbox, and I want to have zero, it is easier to take care of the ones I need to handle immediately, delete the others, and put emails I can't take care of or need immediately into folders. For example, if I buy a plane ticket for a trip the next month, I put the emails into a travel folder so they are not cluttering my inbox.

You are armed with a plan to quit your addictions and time-wasting habits. You have a list of areas you can improve in your life. Now you can literally always keep your goals in sight. On to the final step. In Part IV, we will talk about how to find your passion and follow it. You need to find something you are passionate about that you can focus the majority of your attention on. We'll talk a bit about happiness as well, that elusive state of being that we all strive for, which can, ironically, lead us to unhappiness.

PART IV

FINDING YOUR PASSION AND THOUGHTS ON HAPPINESS

FINDING YOUR PASSION

- If you don't know what your passion is, make it your new passion to find a passion.
- You can have more than one.
- It is normal for your passions to change over time.

You will never find the treasure if you don't dig.

Some people are born knowing they want to be a doctor, athlete, parent, or astronaut. If you know exactly what your passion is, you can go all in, and focus all your energy toward chasing that dream.

What about the rest of us? If you do not know what your absolute passion is in life, that is fine. And in my opinion, this is and should be the most exciting time of your life. Anything is possible! This is where you can spread out your interests using F.P. Messy. Maybe you find you have a long-lost interest in finance or helping people you never even thought about. Start chasing after things you are interested in and eliminating things that you realize are not your passion.

Keep trying new things if you have no idea what you want to do. Don't go to college until you know exactly what you want to spend thousands of dollars on to make a living. Move jobs, learn what you like and don't like. Take notes. Set a time limit for each job (i.e., one year), and don't get stuck somewhere unless you truly love it. Don't just pick jobs that you can easily get, and don't stay in the same field—making a move from one restaurant to another probably will not give you any new insight on what you like or dislike in life.

Be humble. Take shitty jobs and do those jobs like it is the most important thing in the world.

When we are young, we can easily lose sight of some of our passions or be completely discouraged because, at the time, we were not successful. I used to love reading until high school when we were forced into required reading. Luckily I found my love for reading in my twenties again because I was able to choose books that interested me. Reading became fun again and not a chore.

Same with drawing pictures. At some point I realized that I would never make a career as an artist, and I gave up drawing altogether. How I wish I would have continued to draw and improve throughout my life. Think how much better I could be now. Now drawing at least one picture a month is a goal and although it is very hard and I am not very talented, it is so much fun! Don't be afraid to dig up old passions that you may have failed to do well in the past. A passion doesn't mean you have to make money off of it. It can just be something that you do for pleasure.

Don't ever settle for anything. Don't ever settle for a life you don't want, a job you don't love, or a relationship that doesn't make you completely happy.

Refuse to live a normal life. Live the best life you can imagine.

WRITE DOWN your perfect life, listening to your good ego. What do you want to do? Why do you want to do it? If you are saying you don't know what you would want to do, that is fine. Just think of the most amazing life you can imagine. I have never been able to see into my future, maybe you can? What did you like to do as a kid? Maybe that is still your passion.

Write what you wanted to be as a child. It does not matter how stupid it sounds. I wanted to be Indiana Jones and live like *Swiss Family Robinson*. Now, I travel all over the world and have adventures, have ridden an ostrich near Nairobi (like they did in *SFR*), lived on a sailboat, and camped on over a dozen deserted beaches. I am still searching for my island to build my treehouse on. If you wanted to be a superhero, maybe you are meant to be a paramedic or someone else who saves lives. Or if you love romantic comedies, maybe your passion is to be a great parent or spouse. Just remember that life will never be exactly like these movies we all love.

A lot of books mention vision boards. Here is my problem with vision boards. They tell you to put your dreams and goals on a board that you look at every day. They say put your dream house, car, person, money, and jewelry on the board. These objects are not your passions! You need to find out what your true passions are. Would a car or jewelry really make you happy?

Would a big house or unlimited money really make you happy? Don't ask your evil little ego, you need to find this out before you end up like most people who fulfill their "dreams," only to say, "Now what?" People lie about how happy their life is. Don't listen to someone else and try to imitate their life. Or maybe they really are living their dream life. There is nothing wrong with wanting or having cars, houses, or things. But it doesn't mean that is what would make you happy.

How do you find your passion? Never stop searching. I am still chasing my passions and enjoying the ride. I love everything about being a pilot, but it is not my passion. I love writing, but it is not my passion. I love to travel, that *is* one of my passions. You don't have to know exactly what your passion is. Just do what you have always loved. I find new passions all the time, and others fade away. If you love basketball, then coach a Little League team. If you love to cook, cook. Use your imagination to incorporate your passions into your life. If you like to build or fix things, start a side business or just do it for fun.

Finding your purpose in life. Most people do not find their purpose: it will either find you, or through your passions your purpose will eventually become clear. I believe for the majority of us, our purpose is to be good parents and raise a nice family. I still have not figured out what my purpose is yet. I don't lay awake at night worrying about it either. It is exciting not knowing what my purpose is. Maybe it is just to have a family and raise kids while sailing around the world? That would be amazing!

Don't quit your day job…yet. If you are miserable at your job, come up with an escape-from-jail plan. Run some numbers. How much money would you need to quit your job and chase your passion? Don't go into debt or steal, but if something is really your passion, you can find a way to achieve it.

That said, planning doesn't mean you *don't* act. Don't use planning as an excuse to never actually do what you want to do. There is no plan too outrageous; anything is possible. I meet people all the time while traveling who have quit their job, sold everything, and started a completely new life following their dreams. Not one of them has regretted their decision. Some found entirely new lifestyles. Others realized they actually enjoyed their previous job, and were looking forward to going back into the same field. Either way, their dream gave them clarity on the life they wanted to lead.

This is where most people probably will make the most excuses. Everyone thinks it would be stupid or impossible to quit their job and chase some crazy dream. But maybe you don't have to quit your job. What could you do to make more time in your life to chase your passions? Is the location you are in holding you back? Have you ever dreamed of living somewhere else? Have you ever applied for a job there? Here is the secret formula.

Get rid of whatever is holding you back.
+
Sell all your stuff.
+
Move to your ideal location.
=
Freedom!

It is not easy to initiate this, but it really is so simple once you have done it. I've done it three times. I meet people all over the world who have done it. How do you know if you are having crazy thoughts, or if this is really your dream? Crazy thoughts go away in less than a few days. Your crazy dreams stay with you. They never go away. These are your true dreams not wanting to die!

No matter what, you have to start actively pursuing your passion. Release all fears. You cannot fail. A failure would only mean you were chasing the wrong passion. A failure will only be the realization of your new direction in life.

If you think life is unfair to you and you are in your darkest moment and you don't know how to get out…this is the best time of your life. I really mean it. If you feel completely lost in life, remember this should be the most exciting time. Because only then do you have every imaginable door out there open to you. This is do or die, you have nothing to lose. If you stay in your current position, you will continue down the same path and hopefully find a way to be comfortable. But if you seek a new life, a life with less comfort and more risk, this is where it gets interesting. This is your chance to do something amazing. And if you fail, who cares? You can always go back to your old, comfortable life knowing you at least tried.

People will not support your dream. All you need is you. Don't listen to other people's excuses or reasons why it wouldn't work. We are constantly pressured by the media, friends, and family to live a certain life that they think would be best for us. It is only out of love, and they want to see us safe and happy and successful. But they can't see the crazy dreams in our head being achievable because that is not their passion. Learn how to think, not what to think. Follow *your* inner desires. There is no right way to live. That being said, make sure you have a good plan and have done your research before doing anything too irresponsible.

Great ideas. We all have great ideas sometimes that we get excited about. But before you quit your job to follow a passion, try it out first. This happened to me while writing this book. I got so excited when I finished the first rough draft that I started an LLC, made a website, started an email list, and read two books on how to start social media campaigns. I also had all these great ideas for a YouTube channel. Then when it came time to make the videos, I realized I hate myself on camera. I hate editing. I hate social media. When it came time to actually put in the work, I realized this was not something I could be passionate about.

Try things before you get too excited about them. Starting a business is a lot harder and a lot more work than having a cool name and a great idea. I'm not trying to kill anyone's dream— just find out if it is really something you are so passionate about that you are willing to put in all the work it would take. No one gets rich because they had a good idea; they get rich because they worked their ass off.

Your life is not a song. In almost every movie, show, or song out there is a really horrible message being planted into your brain. I love all kinds of music, I like watching movies occasionally, but remember to enjoy it for what it is and know it is not reality. All the love songs and most movies send a message of desperation, jealousy, and a false hope of true love. Think of all the movies guys like to watch, *Rambo*, *Die Hard*. These all teach us anger, revenge, and violence are what a real man is. How many movies portray the rich as stuck-up a-holes? It leaves us no motivation to become better because we do not want to be a-holes. Most comedies portray the funny guy as someone who is a complete bum. Living with his parents, no job, lazy, but loveable and funny. Learn to separate reality from fiction, and don't fall for false narratives.

Search for unique jobs. Imagine your dream job. No matter how ridiculous it is, it may be out there. If it isn't, why not be the first person to open a frog rescue? I've always wanted to brag to people about having a rescue frog.

Attractive woman: "That's a cute frog, Eric."

Me: "Thanks, it's a rescue."

I meet all kinds of fascinating people while traveling. Who knew there were so many interesting and different ways to make money? Search for a job that can open new doors and ways of thinking. This will take some research, creative thinking, and talking to other people. Here is a list of interesting jobs that people I met traveling either worked while traveling or worked to fund their travels:

- Fruit picker in Australia
- English teacher in a foreign country
- California marijuana picker
- Scuba dive instructor anywhere there is a beautiful beach town
- Crew on a yacht
- Oil rig worker
- Global dog sitter

- Forest ranger in Canada who only works summers and spends winters in Mexico
- Volunteer, hostel employee, bartender, flight attendant, and so many more!

Timing. There is a fine line between living your best life now and planning and saving for the future. You have to figure out if your dreams can wait. If your passion is fishing, most likely when you retire, the fish will still be there. But what about the more complex dreams that may not be achievable later in life? Traveling is something that you can do when you're sixty-five, but will you still want to take the same trips? If you want to take a trip around Europe, then sure, you can delay your travels. But there is no way I would still go on some of my past crazy adventures. Decide if it is better to act now and follow your passions, or to pursue them with the future in mind. Ask yourself, "Will my dreams still be there when I retire? Will I still want to do those dreams at my retirement age?"

What about me? Thanks for asking. Most recently, I have my dream job, I am out of debt, I have my dream truck (2014 Silverado), I am making more money than I ever imagined I would. I *had* a condo on the beach in Florida, I *had* a cabin in Georgia, I was traveling every month with my beautiful and successful fiancé. But I found myself unhappy. I had fallen into the normal life I never wanted.

I fought it hard. I told myself (maybe my evil little ego speaking) that I was living the dream. I had a life most people would love to have. But I couldn't lie to myself. I was living someone else's dream. The hardest part was leaving a girl I loved, whose family I loved, who I wanted to make happy more than anything.

But I had to leave her. I knew if I didn't chase my crazy dream of writing a book, retiring early, and sailing around the world looking for my *Swiss Family Robinson* treehouse, I would end up unfulfilled. I wouldn't be happy, and I wouldn't be able to make her happy.

Most people probably think I'm either selfish, stupid, crazy, or all three. I'm simply following my passions and chasing my dreams. Now I am homeless, but it's not that bad. I've made Zanzibar, Sri Lanka, Thailand, Hawaii, and Mexico my home since I've been "homeless." And I've spent some time in Ohio with family and friends that was long overdue. The important thing is that I'm chasing my dreams. I may realize I don't want to live in a treehouse someday, but that's okay; it just means I've found a new passion.

Advice from Eric Island. When I was a kid, I used to think people were saying human *beans* instead of human *beings*. So I came up with these words of…wisdom?

You are a human bean, waiting to be planted and grown. What kind of bean are you? What do you want to grow into?

GBL CHALLENGE

Write down right now, if you were on your deathbed at this exact moment, what would you wish you would have done or tried? Fill in the blanks: I wish I would have tried to _____.

Now put those things on the top of your GBL Plan and start working toward them.

THOUGHTS ON HAPPINESS

I want to share with you a few thoughts on one of the most misused terms in self-help books or media: happiness. Most of us chase this dream of happiness without fully understanding that it is not a final destination. You can't *find* happiness. It's not hidden under a rock or at the end of a rainbow. It's not in any book. It's just another temporary feeling like loneliness or boredom. Here's what I learned.

The worst goal I ever made. To be happy. The problem is it is too broad. What does that mean, to be happy? I thought it meant to find a way to be happy all the time. This led to drinking too much, smoking, really all my bad habits and addictions. We have to learn to accept temporary moments of unhappiness. Happiness is not a constant state of mind you can reach. Learn to accept there will be times when you don't feel happy. You don't need anything to make you feel better. Just accept you will be temporarily in a state of boredom, anxiety, loneliness, etc.

The key to happiness is the pursuit of happiness. Do something. Do whatever you can every day to get a step closer to your dream. It's like winning a championship in sports. It's great to win, but then what? Are you automatically happy for the rest of your life because your team won the championship? Do you quit watching your team next year? Do you stop practicing next year? No, the fun is the challenge of the entire season.

Vacations are another example. Isn't it great to have an exciting trip planned that you can't stop thinking about? You probably are so excited and motivated you set really shitty goals, like losing twenty pounds in a month! (How did that work out?) So even if you managed to lose twenty pounds and have a great vacation, chances are you will not be happy for the rest of your life because of this. (And you will probably gain the weight back during vacation, anyway.) The happiness doesn't last.

You can't think achieving a goal or making everything on your vision board come true will make you happy. Enjoy the challenges you are facing. When you conquer them, look forward to new challenges!

Do not ever say, "I'll be happy when I _____." Pay off the house, get a new car, get a new job, get married, etc. You will only be happy when you realize you already have what it takes to be happy. You have a life, a body, and you can breathe. Add in some challenges for yourself and start working hard toward them, and you will most likely see an increase in happiness.

You will not always be happy. Another key to happiness is understanding and accepting this fact. You will have moments, days, even years or decades, filled with anger, sorrow, tragedy, sickness, boredom, heartbreak, and more. But you can remain hopeful throughout these lows in your life by knowing it will someday pass. And you can manage the struggles by having a plan and sticking to the plan.

Falling into the trap of a normal life. I woke up one morning realizing I fell into the very trap I worked so hard not to fall into! I had everything a normal person would have been happy with. I tried to be a normal person. But it didn't work, I was not happy living the life that most people would love to have.

The scary thing is we are good at adapting to situations. Give your life a check every so often. Are you living *your* dream life, or someone else's? It's okay to live a normal life if that is your dream. If you want to live a comfortable life, I'll still be your friend. But if your ideal life is not what the Joneses are doing, then don't try to live like them!

Don't let other people influence the way you are. People told me all the time when I was growing up that I was quiet and shy. It is true that I am an introvert. I am quiet and shy in a lot of ways. But because people told me this, I thought I had to act that way. One of the things I hated when people would say was, "Oh look! Eric is coming out of his shell today!" It made me want to crawl back in my shell and never come out again.

During my youth, I was one thousand times more quiet and shy than I really am. Then I moved away for college, found alcohol, and became something else I really am not: the life of the party! I am still working on finding a balance between the quiet and shy Eric, while also coming out of my shell. Ugh, I hate that! What am I, a freaking turtle?!

Stop complaining! Most people in the US are living better than kings did one hundred years ago. Most bums in the US live better than 27 percent of the world's population. I made up that statistic, but from my travels, it seems to be true. Have you ever been somewhere where the people have nothing? Jungle, village, small town. Why do those people always seem happier and less stressed? Our egos mixed with all the marketing thrown at us every day make us think we need a whole lot more than we really do to make our lives meaningful and happy.

Do not become angry or worry about things you cannot control. If you ever want to see an example of this, become a gate agent at an airport. You will see it numerous times every day. People absolutely flip out when *their* flight is delayed. If *their* flight is canceled, look out!

Remember, life will go on even after things completely ruin our plans. Oh, and if you are a gate agent: respect. And I'm sure this is the case for most people who work in any kind of public relations or service. So be nice to people and realize it is probably not the fact that they hate you that *your* flight was canceled, or there was mustard on your burger. The spit? Yeah, they hate you.

Stop thinking your life is not fair. Life is unfair to all of us equally. Life is not fair. But in a way, it is fair because everyone's life is not fair. Does that make sense? Good!

I believe we are all given a chance in life to be the best possible person. Don't look at another person's life with envy. Only focus on what you can control. Everyone has to find out their own path in life. It doesn't matter what situation you were born into. *Everyone has issues.* We are very good at putting on a happy face when we are around others because we want people to believe we are happy. It is good to put on a happy face and not spoil everyone else's day because no one wants to be around Mr. Grumpy. However, we must realize that just because we feel certain negative feelings and everyone else seems to be doing so great, it doesn't mean that we are the only ones who feel this way. Everyone suffers in some way. Some show it, others tell you about it. Most of us hide it. We all need to actively try to fix our issues.

Might not be your fault (example: abusive parents or not a "cool" kid), but it is your problem. Those are the cards you were dealt. Life is a game. Deal with it.

We all had a friend who would quit a game because it was "not fair." Don't be that kid! You can't win the game if you quit. Keep playing, keep learning, wait for your hand. Be prepared when your opportunity arises and act.

Do not blame your past experiences for the way you are. You can't change the past, you can only heal yourself in the present. For every person out there complaining about their unfair situations in life, there is someone who had a worse situation than you and made it. Quit whining and get busy living.

Stop complaining about your current job or life situation without doing anything about it. So many people at previous companies complained about being stuck at their current job, but how many were actively pursuing another career? Do you complain about your job? Quit. Or start making big moves to get a new job. If no one is hiring now, get your shit together so when they do, you are ready.

Quit being a baby. I can call out babies because they can't complain about it being offensive. All they can do is cry and be helpless. Did your parents or friends ever tell you to stop acting like a baby? Babies are supposed to cry. It is the only way they can communicate until a certain age. They do not have a way of knowing when the next meal will come or telling you they just crapped their diaper and need a little help, so they cry to let their parents know they need something.

Fortunately, when we grow older, we don't still cry like a baby, but whining is the grown-up form of this. We whine when something doesn't go our way. Learn to deal with life's unpredictability. Stop crying.

Stop being offended. Don't take everything personally. Most people are not trying to offend you on purpose. If they are, remove those people from your life.

Finding the right person cannot make you happy. No one can make you happy. If you are not happy to begin with, no person can fix that. Yes, at first it will be exciting, and they will be a great distraction from your problems, but ultimately no one can change your happiness. A goal cannot be to find the right person. You need to become the person that your dream person would want to date. The only person who can make you happy is you.

For every single person out there who desperately wants to find a mate, there is someone in a relationship who desperately wants to get out.

Making someone else happy will not make you happy. This

is where guys make a joke and say, "Happy wife, happy life." I really hope you are only joking. Of course, you want to keep your spouse happy, but it needs to be mutual. Subtracting from your happiness to add happiness to someone else's life does not equal greater happiness. Simple maths. Find someone who shares the same crazy dreams as you.

Do not focus on the past. Do not have regrets, only life lessons. If you spend your time thinking about how you have wasted all those years, take that as a lesson, and then get out there and do whatever it is you have been regretting you didn't do. Or if the opportunity is simply not possible anymore, then just let it go. Don't let something from the past ruin or control your life, or even your day.

You must accept that you will fail in life. You will not get accepted to what you think would have been your dream job, you will smoke a cigarette when you are drunk, you will eat an entire crave case at Taco Bell on your diet. Do not let these brief moments of weakness discourage you. Get back on your game plan.

Jungle wisdom. Life will always throw shit at you. You have to fight back. Don't take that shit. (Literally, monkeys will throw poop at you. Keep some little rocks in your pocket, or something to fight back.)

Put your life on silent mode. At least once a day, get to know who you really are with no outside influence. Start out small if you need to. Take one minute with no television, no phone, no social media, no newspapers, no talking, no gossip. It is truly amazing. Add this to your MGFD list.

Never stop learning. Most people stop learning after they get out of school. You think you learned all you need to know for your life and career, you are grown-up and kind of responsible now, and then you stop learning. I hate when parents say, "I learn so much from my kids!" Really? Aren't you supposed to be teaching them? I get it, they mean their kids are cute, and they are amazed how smart they are. But seriously, you shouldn't have too much to learn from your kids. Keep learning. Don't always rely on old advice.

Smile :) Some of my favorite moments in life were on days when I was completely down in the dumps, and a random person gave me a really big smile. This happened to me recently in Mexico, in a small town where the locals there were not as fortunate as most of us in the USA. I was stressed out over a million things and feeling like a failure because my publishers (who I love now) hadn't contacted me in a while. I was feeling like a complete failure, like a loser who thought he was stupid for even thinking he could write a book. I felt even worse thinking about how I just wrote the book on how to change your life, get busy living, and be happy…and I wasn't happy.

It was siesta time in the little beach town, and no one else was on the street. When I turned the corner, a severely handicapped person, all by themselves, walked past me and gave me the biggest smile and goofy wave. Wow, did that make me feel like an ass for worrying about my stupid problems. But at the same time, it made me realize how stupid I was for worrying about problems out of my control and not being thankful for all the things I did have. A random smile can seriously change someone's day.

GBL CHALLENGE

Next time you randomly come in contact with Mr. Grumpy, try giving him your biggest smile and just say hello. It could change his whole day. If you think you don't have a beautiful smile, I think every smile is equally amazing. My favorite smiles are the ones that come from people who don't have a perfect dental-commercial smile.

THE END...OF THE BEGINNING

Our time together is almost done. I would like to leave you with a recap of everything covered in the book and some final words of motivation. Thanks so much for reading, and I hope when you finish this book, it will be an exciting new beginning to a new and improved life!

FINAL WORDS OF MOTIVATION

This is the world against you. Guess what? You do not have very much competition. Just look around you. Don't turn on the television, don't look on social media. Go to Walmart, walk around your town, pay attention to the people around you at work. If you simply exchange a few time-wasting bad habits and start new habits to improve your life, you will already be on your way to the top. This is not so you can walk around with your nose in the air looking down on everyone. This is to make *you* feel better about yourself and Franklin Patrick F-ing Messy. When you are at your best, you will make everyone around you better and happier.

Do you feel like your life is at a dead end, and there is no way out? Like you have nothing to live for? If you feel like life is impossible to get through without a crutch or something to help take away your pain, I hope you can form a plan to bring meaning to your life. I hope you can find new (or old) passions to exchange what you do when you have temporary feelings of discomfort, fear, anxiety, or depression. Remember, you are simply delaying your misery until tomorrow every time you fall back on your crutch. We need to get to the root of our problems. Face your past. Own it, embrace it, forgive it. Whatever you have to do, don't be a prisoner to those feelings anymore.

Maybe you are feeling like your life couldn't be better. Well excuse me, Mr. Perfect! Hopefully you found something in this book or thought of something you could improve on. If you can't, may I recommend reading a book on narcissism?

Every day we are presented with a simple choice. Get busy living, or get busy dying. What will you choose? Will you make choices that will incrementally improve the quality of your future life, or will you choose to slowly fade away into a life of comfort? Almost all of us can choose what to do with our lives. You might think you have to go to work tomorrow morning to survive. (It's probably a good idea. Don't ever do anything rash without having a plan first.) But what if you did something tomorrow that would allow you to leave that job you despise in a month or a year? Where could you be in a year if today you started planning your escape?

If you feel like the world hates you and everything and everyone is against you, you are wrong. The world doesn't care about you. It is nobody's job to look after us after a certain age. The world is waiting for you to make a move. Someone is out there waiting for you to join their company, someone is out there who wants you to start a company (I still want my damn rescue frog), someone is out there who wants you to get your shit together so they can love you.

Stop waiting for the right moment. That moment is now!

GBL PLAN REVIEW

Here's a review of what this book has covered.

QUITTING ADDICTIONS AND BAD HABITS:

- Identify your problem.
- Identify your triggers and create a contingency plan for your triggers.
- Figure out what excuses you are making.
- Make a pros and cons list.
- Keep track of your failures. Remember, every failure is a victory toward killing The Beast.
- Form a game plan to quit and then never quit quitting. Try every method out there. Have faith you will quit.
- Remember the GBL conundrum:

Bad habits—Difficult to form. Difficult to quit.

Good habits—Easy to form. Easy to break.

CREATE A QUALITY LIFESTYLE:

- Take a good look at F.P. Messy: Financial, Physical, Mental,

Emotional, Spiritual, Social, You (Your Passions). Write down where you want to improve, and what your goals are.

THE GBL PLAN:

- Ask yourself questions: What are your priorities, fears, and excuses? How can you overcome them? Did I win/get better today?
- Make a list of F.P. Messy ideas (go ahead and borrow from "Create a Quality Lifestyle").
- Set periodic goals (MGFD, but also daily, monthly, yearly, lifetime, and achievements).
- Create a mission statement and mantras and assign values you want to live by.

PUTTING IT ALL TOGETHER:

- Write everything down: triggers and contingency plans, your pros and cons list, and the GBL Plan. Type it out. Print it out.
- Keep this piece of paper with you at all times. Read it. Read it again. Read it every time you have a slight feeling of discomfort or any negative thoughts. Read it in the morning and before you go to bed. Keep it in your pocket. Have a copy with you at all times.

I hope this book finds you when you are ready to quit your old life, start fresh, and get busy living. If you are not ready, start preparing yourself, little by little. What is one thing could you do? What habit do you want to quit? Just start writing down every time you have a craving. Write down every time you quit and relapse.

I have never been able to look very far in the future. I couldn't imagine my lungs failing me from forty years of smoking. I couldn't imagine not being happy on a minimum wage job thirty years from when I was twenty-five years old. I couldn't imagine that drinking eighteen beers would make me feel like crap the next morning.

If you are like me, and you have no worry or fear about the future, here is what I do to stay motivated in life. Set things in the near future that you can look forward to. For me, I love to travel, so I always have a trip planned. It keeps me focused and motivated toward that next trip. Find something you love or have always wanted to do and figure out a way, right now, that you could make this a reality in the near future. You don't have to travel somewhere exotic. Find a new place in your home state you have never been to before. Go to a concert or festival. Plan a hike in nature. If you are feeling depressed about your life, go volunteer at a homeless shelter or talk to some old people at a retirement home. Have something to look forward to in the near future. Do something you are afraid to do. Face your fears.

The key to this book is having a plan that you can fall back on in hard times. Life will always be full of distractions. We will fall off our workout plan, start-up bad habits, gain weight, lose sight of our priorities in life, and lose sight of our true passions in life. Set up a new mindset. Tell yourself everyday will be a challenge. Every day it's you against the world. Looking at your GBL Plan daily will give you a daily reminder of what is really important in your life. Follow your plan, don't give up, get back on track when you go astray.

There will be times when you need to buckle down and focus all your attention on something else, a family situation, studying for a new job, or maybe you just wake up one day and realize you have been on a bender for the last week. It is easy to lose track of our lives. Now, when you fall out of your routine, you can have in the back of your mind all the things you want to do to make your life the best possible—that's why a written plan is so important.

Even if your life is going great, you still want to have a reminder of all the things you want to do. Bucket lists don't work because you probably don't look at them every day, and it is probably a list made up of exciting things other people have done. This is *your* Get Busy Living Plan. Everything in your plan should be what *you* want to do to make your life, and those around you, better.

Time and a body. Two things every human on the planet is given for free. Don't waste either one of these. Go on, get busy living!

Let me leave you with a story that will always stay with me. As a passenger on a long flight to Tanzania, after landing, this kid in the row in front of me shakes his brother awake and says excitedly, "Wake up, buddy, this is our new life now!" I'm usually not a guy who thinks things kids say are cute (I still have *some* Rambo in me), but this became one of my new mottos. Figure out your game plan, and wake up tomorrow morning and tell yourself…

Wake up, buddy, this is our new life now!

FINAL GBL CHALLENGE

Tomorrow morning, I challenge you to wake up and do one small thing before anything else. Something so little it only takes a minute or less. Ten push-ups, make your bed, whatever. Start your day with a win. Ask yourself how it feels to start the day with a win. Good, now build on that. Find something you can do before bed that is equally simple. Watch one less TV show and go to bed early, or write one sentence in a journal. Try to get better every day. Win. Every. Day.

AN INVITATION TO THE GET BUSY LIVING CLUB!

We get excited about books we read. I wanted to become a real estate mogul after reading *Rich Dad Poor Dad*, and I bought a nice bike and wanted to start racing after reading *It's Not About the Bike* by Lance Armstrong. The point of this book is to motivate you to live a more fulfilling life.

But before you quit your job tomorrow or leave your spouse and kids to start a frog rescue, send me an email. Your family and friends will try to protect you in a certain way. I care more about your dreams. It saddens me to see people living a life of unfulfilled dreams. I want to help. And hopefully there is a way to fulfill your dreams, keep your job, and keep your family!

So reach out to me at gbl@getbusylivingclub.com. You already bought the book, so I want to thank you by helping you figure out the best game plan for your life. Send me your list of excuses. Why you can't quit your bad habits, why you can't follow your dreams. I will try my best to help you with more nonprofessional advice.

However, nothing is FREE! By reaching out to me, I can learn how this book is helping people, and also what isn't working for you, so someday maybe I can write *GBL 2.0* or *GBL for Introverts and Unicorns*.

If you're someone who thrives in a community, you can also join the Get Busy Living Club at getbusylivingclub.com and subscribe to my weekly newsletter to get even more information on how to face your fears, chase your passions, and live your life to the fullest. There was so much I left out because I wanted to keep this book short. But I hope to form a community where we all can help each other improve our lives. Let's get better together.

A SHORT LIST OF THANK YOUS

Thanks to the entire Scribe Team. From the first phone call with Miles Rote, I knew this was going to be the right decision for me. Thank you, Miles, for making me feel comfortable with investing in Scribe. I learned so much from the Scribe School videos, and everyone I talked to throughout the process was absolutely amazing. Special thanks to my publication managers, Katie Villalobos and Ryan Garcia, for making this a fun and enjoyable process. And also special thanks to my structural editor, Tashan Mehta, you were awesome, and I couldn't have asked for a better person to work with!

I would also like to thank Mark Chait for the initial edit, great advice, and much appreciated confidence boost. Thanks to my line editor, Melissa Jo Clapp, for cleaning up my C+ public high school writing errors. It is the little things that matter. (Who knew that there are actually two *t*'s in quitting?) And thank you to the entire team in title, cover, layout, and graphics.

Thanks to my proofreaders Caroline Hough and Aviva Gellman for cleaning up the entire book. Thanks to Vi La Bianca for helping with the final title and subtitle, without their expertise, I would still be trying to decide on the subtitle!

David Edmondson (soulsnapss.com), a professional photographer who I met at a yoga retreat in Mexico the same day I found out I needed professional photos for my author bio. Nice timing! My simulator partner during captain upgrade, Captain Mike Heuring, for the idea to put mustard on veggies. Captain Kevin Burke for introducing me to Bitcoin and the world of crypto and indirectly introducing me to Scribe. Azam and Patricia from Toronto for all their advice during a strange time in my life. (Wait, I thought I was the one writing the self-help book!) Haha.

To Mike in Thailand who let me be a hermit during my three-week writing spree at his Airbnb.

The entire crew aboard the SV (sailing vessel) Twister: Robert Methorst (the owner and his lovely family and friends), Captain Jakob Zuern, Julia Lykke Sorensen, Dutch Jack Sparrow, Leanne (Irish) Barrett, and Samantha "Zee Manta." There was no better place to finish my book than sailing around the Caribbean on a tall ship! Also thanks to Suzy Van Der Veeken from Ocean Nomads for organizing the trip. If you are interested in sailing check out her awesome community at oceannomads.co.

To all the locations where I did all my final edits:

Present Moment Retreat, Troncones, Mexico (which, ironically, is near Zihuatanejo where Andy talks about going in his "get busy living" quote in *Shawshank Redemption*).

New Grounds Coffee House, Hilliard, Ohio.

Honolulu Coffee at Moana Surfrider, Honolulu, Hawaii.

Ground Central Coffee Company, East Midtown Manhattan, New York City.

Polat Renaissance, Istanbul, Turkey.

Kreol K Fe, Anse L'Ane, Martinique.

And last but not least, to the six people in my life who have always supported (or at least accepted!) all my crazy dreams: Mom, Dad, my sister Andrea, and my niece Cambryn. Bryan and Alicia Cross, my best friend and his wife, who has become like a best friend as well. Love you all.

LIST OF RECOMMENDED BOOKS

Consider *Get Busy Living* your crash course in learning how to enhance your life. I highly recommend reading further about any or all subjects that interest you, or any areas you think you could use improvement. This book is just the tip of the iceberg of the different ways we can improve our life. I wanted to write a book without any science or any real reasoning (it does not mean I didn't research a lot into the science and reasoning behind it). This is a short list of resources that can give you more insight about some of the subjects we have covered. I've never read a bad self-help book—there is always something useful in them. The worst one I ever read gave me confidence that I, too, could write a book! Try searching for the top fifty self-improvement books for men/women/procrastination/emotional health/whatever you want help with for more recommendations.

Quitting addictions—

- *Allen Carr's Easy Way to…*

Quit smoking, drinking, overeating, gambling, caffeine, fear of flying, and more. I have only read the book about smoking, but it is by far the best way, in my opinion, to quit. I imagine the principles are the same for the other addictions.

- *Dopamine Nation: Dopamine Nation: Finding Balance in the Age of Indulgence* by Anna Lembke

Financial—If you are like me and were completely ignorant about all areas related to money, I would start with Ramsey. Most of it is very basic, and it's a good place to start. Not everyone agrees with his approach to get out of debt before anything else, but the key is forming a plan for your money. *Crypto Revolution* is great if you have no idea how crypto works. It simplifies it to the point you still will not really know how it works, but you will be able to form an opinion if you think crypto is a worthy investment.

- *Dave Ramsey's Complete Guide to Money* by Dave Ramsey
- *Rich Dad Poor Dad: What the Rich Teach Their Kids About Money That the Poor and Middle Class Do Not!* by Robert T. Kiyosaki
- *Crypto Revolution: Bitcoin, Cryptocurrency, and the Future of Money* by Sam Volkering

Physical—There are a million diets and workout plans out there. I think the key is finding foods you like that are healthy. The diet I follow the closest is The Abs Diet (which has nothing to do with getting six- pack abs). There is a men's and women's version.

- *The Abs Diet: The Six-Week Plan to Flatten Your Stomach and Keep You Lean for Life* by David Zinczenko and Ted Spiker

Mental—If you want to learn how to learn, read *Limitless*. If you are like me and feel different from most people, read *Veronika*. Maybe only the sane people live inside the nuthouse?

- *Limitless: Upgrade Your Brain, Learn Anything Faster, and Unlock Your Exceptional Life* by Jim Quik
- *Veronika Decides to Die* by Paulo Coelho

Emotional—

- *Courage: The Joy of Living Dangerously* by Osho
- *Quiet: The Power of Introverts in a World That Can't Stop Talking* by Susan Cain

Social—I wish I could recommend more books for the feminine folks in this area, but a quick search for the best books for women for relationships should put you on the right track. *Captivate* is a great beginner book for learning how to communicate better. If you are in a relationship, or especially if you are currently not in a relationship, I highly recommend reading books about the opposite sex. I don't mean books on how to be a pick-up artist or how to trick the other sex into liking you. Find books that will teach you how to understand the opposite sex or how to be a better partner.

- *Captivate: The Science of Succeeding with People* by Vanessa Van Edwards
- *The Way of the Superior Man: A Spiritual Guide to Master-

ing the Challenges of Women, Work, and Sexual Desire by David Deida

Spiritual—If you are not offended by language, listen to the Affirmations on YouTube. Absolutely hilarious and motivating at the same time. Rambo listens to this!

- *The Miracle of Mindfulness: An Introduction to the Practice of Meditation* by Thich Nhat Hanh
- *Zen Mind, Beginner's Mind: Informal Talks on Zen Meditation and Practice* by Shunryu Suzuki
- *I AM Affirmations—F*ck Procrastination and All Excuses* by PowerThoughts Meditation Club

Finding Your Passion and Purpose—*7 Habits* is also good for writing a mission statement and finding values. Barbara Sher is great for finding your passion/purpose.

- *I Could Do Anything If Only I Knew What It Was* by Barbara Sher
- *A New Earth: Awakening to Your Life's Purpose* by Eckhart Tolle
- *The 7 Habits of Highly Effective People* by Stephen R. Covey
- *The Alchemist* by Paulo Coelho

Other—If you think traveling is something you can only do if you are rich, think again. Read *Vagabonding* for many great insights and ways to travel on a small budget. *The Art of Non-Conformity* is a great book about thinking differently about life. *Atomic Habits* is the best-selling book out there right now about setting habits. It's a great book if you want some more science and stories about creating habits. Wim Hof helped me not be such a baby in cold weather. Now I take cold showers daily and enjoy having to fly in Alaska during winter.

- *Ocean Nomad: How to Catch a Ride and Contribute to a Healthier Ocean* by Suzanne Van Der Veeken
- *The Art of Non-Conformity: Set Your Own Rules, Live the Life You Want, and Change the World* by Chris Guillebeau
- *The Compound Effect* by Darren Hardy
- *Vagabonding: An Uncommon Guide to the Art of Long-Term World Travel* by Rolf Potts
- *Atomic Habits: An Easy & Proven Way to Build Good Habits & Break Bad Ones* by James Clear
- *The Wim Hof Method: Activate Your Full Human Potential* by Wim Hof
- Any book by Tim Ferriss

ABOUT THE AUTHOR

ERIC TRAUGH is a Boeing 747 captain from Columbus, Ohio. He has lived in Florida for the last eighteen years. He has spent the last fifteen years traveling the world and researching traditional and nontraditional ways to overcome addictions and the true meaning of happiness. In the future, he hopes to start a family and sail around the world.

Spoiler alert on the next page if you have not watched *The Shawshank Redemption*.

"I find I'm so excited I can barely sit still or hold a thought in my head. I think it's the excitement only a free man can feel. A free man at the start of a long journey. Whose conclusion is uncertain. I hope I can make it across the border. I hope the Pacific is as blue as it is in my dreams. I hope."

—RED (MORGAN FREEMAN),
THE SHAWSHANK REDEMPTION

www.ingramcontent.com/pod-product-compliance
Lightning Source LLC
Chambersburg PA
CBHW060525080526
44586CB00012B/610